A Game Development Primer

Faisal Qureshi

Table of Contents

About the Author

Faisal Qureshi is the founder and manager of Fiz-rand Entertainment LLC. Faisal has been a professor for game and simulation development and has published articles such as "Immersion, The Greatest Hook" and has given talks for conferences for various game related topics. With a master's degree in computer engineering from Columbia University, Faisal remains an active member of the gaming community.

Introduction

With the video game industry being a multi-billion dollar industry with a huge market and constant technological advances being made, it is definitely something that cannot be overlooked. This book covers various elements of game development ranging from design to programming to other factors that are included in game development. From a design perspective, interface design, character development, storytelling, and level design are covered. The book also covers basic C++ programming and object-oriented programming in C++. Finally, topics such as audio in games, artificial intelligence, simulations, and networking in games are also included in the book as well as the development process and methodologies. This book is primarily intended for aspiring game developers who want to know what it is all about.

Chapter 1: Game Design I

The Birth of Gaming

Interactive digital entertainment started in two primary institutions. They were first created by individuals who were a part of academia and the military. In academia, at the Massachusetts Institute of Technology, Steve Russell developed *Spacewar!* in 1961. *Spacewar!* Was one of the first interactive computer game. With the emergence of *Spacewar!*, Nolan Bushnell took the idea of the game and ported it to arcade. He also founded the still present company called Atari and the first Atari game, Pong, was released in 1972.

On the other side, Martin Bromely provided coin-operated entertainment for the military. It was he who had started SEGA in 1952. SEGA or "SEvice GAmes of Japan" has, like Atari, survived till current day. SEGA's role in the industry has varied over time. In regards to hardware, SEGA had initially released the SEGA Mastersystem, followed by the SEGA Genesis/Megadrive, followed by SEGA CD, Saturn, and Dreamcast. Despite being a console manufacturer, SEGA has also had an active role in software from which emerged the infamous Sonic the hedgehog.

Other major players of the gaming industry today that also were established early in the history of gaming were names such as Activision, Midway, Namco, and Nintendo. Midway had developed *Galaga* and is also known for the *Mortal Kombat* hit. Namco was the developer for *Pac-Man*. The innovation of *Pac-Man* was that a much larger audience was targeted regarding age and gender. The brilliance of Shigeru Miyamoto as a game designer was revealed early in the history of games as well. He is not only the creator of titles such as Donkey Kong and The *Legend of Zelda*, but changed the industry dramatically. Storylines and character development were key factors that were brought to gaming by Miyamoto. Finally, he introduced a character in Donkey Kong in 1977 that rivals SEGA's Sonic; Mario.

Platforms

Video games exist over multiple types of hardware. In its early stages, people were able to play games in public arcades. The arcade machines were coin-operated. This coin-operation was initiated by SEGA. Till today, public arcades are still popular. Certain types of user interfaces can only be found in an arcade. We will talk about user interfaces later in this book.

Another platform for electronic gaming is the console. In 1972, the first home console was released called the Magnavox Odyssey. After that the Atari VCS/2600 was released. This was a cartridge based console machine. To compete with the Atari 2600 another home console emerged called the Intellivision by Mattel.

In 1985, the first Nintendo was released. The effect of the Nintendo made arcades less popular mainly because people could play games in the comfort of their own homes. Hit titles such as Mario Bros. and The Legend of Zelda have had various manifestations from their original form. To compete with the Nintendo, SEGA released the Master System. Thus the battle began between SEGA and Nintendo. Sonic rivaled Mario, and the Genesis/Megadrive rivaled the Super Nintendo (SNES). The Genesis and SNES were 16-bit machines and the timeframe of 1988 to 1995 was known as the 16-bit era. A bit is simply a value of 0 or 1. A byte is made up of 8 bits. The number of possible values that one byte can represent is 2^8, or 256 possible values based on the combinations of the bits being a 0 or 1. To understand the meaning of the Genesis and SNES being 16-bit consoles, you have to look at the hardware of the machines. It also means that these consoles had 16-bit addressing and processing. Furthermore, this means that these consoles were comprised of 16-bit busses (wires) , a 16-bit ALU (Arithmetic Logic Unit), and 16-bit registers. A 16-bit bus simply means a collection of 16 wires where each wire can transmit data. The ALU is the core of a CPU, or central processing unit, that performs mathematical operations on data it receives. A register is a component that holds data and can be thought of as memory. So, a 16-bit register is one that can store 16 bits of data. Since this was the case, each register could store data of values ranging from 0 through 2^{16} . The system architecture would look something like this:

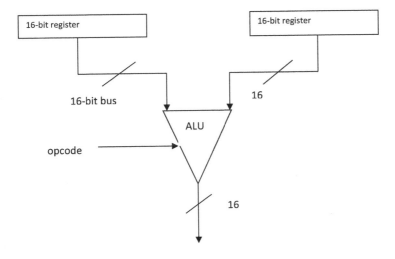

While discussion hardware, it is important to note that the current trend is that hardware is getting cheaper while software is becoming more expensive. If we were to plot out the trend, it would look like this:

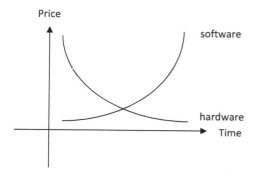

Also, as time has gone on, we have come from low resolution and slow processing, to high resolution and fast processing. This means that games have gotten more complex and there can be a greater sense of realism. As games technology has evolved, we have come from CD based technology to DVD based to Blue-Ray. The primary difference with Blue-Ray is that the blue laser has a smaller width than the common red laser and therefore the Blue-Ray DVD can hold much more data. The color blue has a smaller wavelength than red which makes this possible.

Going back to home consoles, we recently saw the Playstation 2 by Sony, the GameCube by Nintendo, and the Xbox by Microsoft. These are the three giants and hardware vendors that currently own the console market. Today we have the Playstation 3, the Nintendo Wii, and the Xbox 360 from Microsoft.

A third platform for video games is the PC. Initially, there was the Apple II. Sometime afterwards, the Commodore 64 was released with a plethora of 2D games. Commodore also released the Amiga 500 which was an excellent competitor with the SEGA Genesis and the SNES. Many games that came out for the Genesis could also be found for the Amiga 500.

Today, our personal computers can incorporate a CPU, GPU, and a PPU in its architecture. The CPU is a central processing unit where primary calculations and processing occurs. The GPU is the graphics processing unit and handles rendering. Rendering is simply drawing the graphics to the screen. With a GPU, the processing load on the CPU can be alleviated. The PPU is the physics processing unit. The PPU is used for physics calculations such as cloth physics and other physics based effects. Thus, there has been a threefold distribution of processing and calculations for a game which allows the game to run much faster and making the entire system more efficient.

Prior to online play on consoles, PC allowed networked games and a multi-player environment. First, games can be LAN (local area network) based. For LAN games, all players must be on the same subnet. Second, there are online games through the internet. This allows the player to play anywhere there is internet connectivity.   However, today, online and LAN based games are not unique to PC as such capabilities have emerged on consoles.

A fourth platform is handhelds, such as cellular phones and PDAs. This is one reason why 2D games are still viable in today's gaming market. We also have the Gameboy DS by Nintendo, after the Gameboy advanced. There is also the PSP (playstation portable) which has had hit games developed for it such as "God of War: Chains of Olympus". If we look at handhelds a few years back you will find the Atari Lynx, SEGA's Game Gear, and the Nokia N-Gauge.

A Graphics Primer

Although graphics will be discussed in detail later in this book, an introduction to 2D and 3D graphics is an integral part of game design and therefore a primer for it is covered here. The primary difference between 2D and 3D graphics is that 3D graphics incorporate a third axis, a z-axis, on the coordinate system rather than just two axes, namely x and y. So, the comparison would look like this:

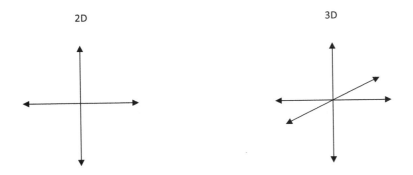

The reason why we have been able to accommodate a z-axis as oppose to earlier 2D games is that we have much more processing power which allows more data to be processed at the same time. With a third axis, there are three coordinates(x,y,z) representing a location rather than just two (x,y) which can be handled much better as computer architecture has evolved. In other words, it is because the graphics is hardware dependent. In terms of motion, in 2D, you have up and down, and left and right. In 3D, you have the 2D motion plus forwards and backwards.

For 2D graphics, which are still used in 3D games for texture mapping, it is important to know how bitmap graphics work. Bitmaps are 2D pixel based graphics. Each pixel on the bitmap is made up of a certain number of bits which determine the color of that pixel. Let us take the example that there is only one bit for each pixel in the bitmap. One bit means two possible values; 0 or 1. The 0 could mean that that pixel will be black and the 1 would mean that that pixel is white. Thus, there are two colors available for use if each pixel is represented by one bit. Your bitmap, showing a black 1, with resolution 5 X 5, may look something like this:

1	1	0	1	1
1	0	0	1	1
1	1	0	1	1
1	1	0	1	1
1	0	0	0	1

To extrapolate on this, we can have x number of bits per pixel. With this there can be 2^x possible colors for that pixel. If we have 8-bit color, that means each pixel can have 1 out of 256 possible colors.

In 3D, the graphics are based on meshes which are based on a collection of triangles (most commonly) where each vertex of the triangle is composed of three components. The components are coordinates for x, y, and z. So the details of each triangle can be determined by nine values together, since a triangle has three vertices.

Vectors are used everywhere in graphics and game development. In 2D, a vector is represented by:

$$V = xi + yj$$

Or

$$V = B_{point} - A_{point}$$

The vector is the two coordinates of point B minus the two coordinates of point A, separately. So, there is an x component and a y component. Graphically, it can be something like this:

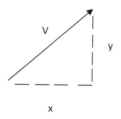

You can find the length, or magnitude, of this vector using Pythagorean theorem, which would be:

$$|V| = sqrt(x^2 + y^2)$$

Now that you understand 2D vectors, we will look at 3D vectors. In 3D, there is an extra coordinate included in the calculations. The vector can be represented as:

$$V = xi + yj + zk$$

Or

$$V = B_{point} - A_{point}$$

To find the magnitude of the 3D vector, an extrapolation of the Pythagorean theorem is used:

$$|V| = sqrt(x^2 + y^2 + z^2)$$

Motivation and Target Audience

People play games for different reasons. Also, when designing a game, it is imperative to know who your target audience is for your game. There are some primary motivational reasons as to why people play games. These five prime reasons are social interaction, physical seclusion, competition, escapism, and challenge. Despite these reasons, games and simply fun to play. After all, it is entertainment.

Social interaction has reached a new level today with digital interactive entertainment due to networks and the internet. People can play, message, and talk to other gamers all around the globe. Due to increased bandwidth and efficiency, MMOGs, or Massively Multiplayer Online Games, are becoming more popular. Some examples of popular MMOGs are Second Life, World of Warcraft, and The Age of Conan. There are also local area network games that can be played at home as LAN parties or at others sites that provide such a service. Whether LAN based, or internet based, human interaction is taking place.

Physical seclusion is also a prime reason why people play games. This is mainly possible with consoles systems. You can play games in the privacy of your homes without any distractions. This is different than when you could only play games at public arcades. The gamer wants to be geographically secluded. However, this does not mean you cannot be social. As mentioned, you can virtually socialize with others online.

People also play games for challenge and competition. The gamer wants to test himself/herself and utilize their skills to overcome various challenges. It is important as a designer not to make the challenges too easy or too hard. If the challenge is too easy, there is no feeling of accomplishment. If the challenge is too hard, the player will get frustrated and not want to play the game anymore. Players who play to win, against the artificial intelligence or other players, usually have a competitive nature.

Finally, the last prime reason why people play games is for escapism. The player wants to get immersed in the virtual world and escape from the "real" world. As a designer, to create an immersive experience many factors must be taken into consideration. The Audio and Visual can enhance the immersive experience, as well as the gameplay, story, and very importantly, the interaction. Immersion is simply getting drawn into the virtual world. As games become more immersive, there is a higher probability of the player of having a place to escape to. Escapism also provides stress-relief. Other forms of media that allow escapism are books and television.

As a designer, you are targeting a certain group of people for your game. The revolutionary feature of Pac-Man was that it appealed to a wider audience than the more common shooters of that time. A designer must take into account the demographics when designer the game. The most critical and greatest distinction between gamers is hardcore and casual gamers. Hardcore gamers are in it for the long haul. Thus, you can make the gameplay more challenging or have higher difficulty modes. The game would usually be longer with more hours of gameplay which allows the story to be more intricate. Casual gamers simply want a "fun-fix" and don't want to spend hours playing the same game. A hardcore gamer would be more interested in *Lost Odyssey* as oppose to *Snake* on a mobile device for casual gamers. Demographics also include gender and age. You have to know whether you are targeting males primarily or females. Also, you need to know what age group you are targeting. For example, you have to know if your game is for children or for teens. It is important to note that these categories are not mutually exclusive as there is some overlap between the divisions. So, some females may play a game that was intended for a male audience, and vice versa. The gaming industry initially was male-dominated but with the introduction of internet based games, more females are emerging in the market.

Game Types and Game Genres

Games can serve various purposes other than the obvious purpose of entertainment. The entertainment comes from the interactive phenomenon, the world immersion, and the emotional engagement. However, games can also be educational, also called edutainment. Games can provide training, called simulations, by simulating real world scenarios such as a flight simulator where a pilot trainee can learn to fly a Boeing 747 with actually being in the aircraft. Games can stimulate community building though online games which allow forms of virtual communication. Finally, games can be used for advertising, also called advergames. These can be seen on the internet as banners or other web pages.

Other than the game's purpose, there are other categories that games can fall in other than the genre of the game. The timing in games is usually divided into two main categories. First, there are games where the timing is in real-time. An example can be sports games. Real-time games require sharp reflexes as there is no concept of "turns". If you do something too late, you could lose life or lose the game. Another example is fighting games such as *Tekken* or *Soul Calibur*. The other type of timing mechanism in games is turn-based. There is no time limit for your actions which allows reflection on what you are about to do. It requires thought, and many times it is against the artificial intelligence, or AI. Role-playing games are primarily turn-based as are some strategy games.

There are different modes you play in for different games. One mode is simply single player. In this mode, only you are playing and no other player is involved. You can also play with other people over local area network, making the game multiplayer. Some games are local multiplayer. This means that you are playing against other players on the same console and not over any sort of network. Finally, there are online games and Massively Multiplayer Online Games, or MMOGs.

For online games, the distinction of types can be further broken down. Online games can be peer-to-peer or based on a client/server architecture. When designing and programming online games, the delays of data communication must be taken into account. There are both pros and cons for peer-to-peer games and also having a client/server architecture. For client/server, there can be a heavy load on the server which is a con because it can cause lag to due high processing. There is also a single point of failure, meaning that if the server goes down you cannot play. Furthermore, there can also be higher delays due to high traffic of incoming requests from the clients. However, the benefit of a client/server model is that the files are centralized and therefore everyone is "on the same page". With peer-to-peer networks there is an issue with security. It also has a decentralized file system which is a con because not everyone may have the same data. Peer-to-Peer networks are good because there are lower delays and thus good for things such as streaming media. When designing a game all these factors need to be taken into account for the best gameplay experience.

Games can be also be distinguished by what genre they fall into. Today, we see a few main genres for games. However, this does not mean that there is no overlap between genres for some games. One genre for games is Action. Action games are "twitch" games where the player needs to react quickly. First Person Shooters and third person shooters usually fall on this category. In first person, the camera is setup to be the eyes of the playable character, or avatar. In third person, the camera is behind the avatar so the gamer can see his or her playable character. In action games, the player is set out to DESTROY ENEMIES!

Another genre is racing games. Examples of popular racing games are *Wipeout*, *Gran Turisimo*, and *Need for Speed*. Fighting games are another genre. In fighting games, the player commonly has a side view of the fight. Also important in fighting games is learning the fighter's moves and combos. Examples of great fighting games are *Mortal Kombat*, *Tekken*, *Street Fighter* series, and *Soul Calibur*.

A fourth genre is adventure. Adventure games usually have an intricate storyline that incorporates a plot, setting, theme, and introduces characters and their persona. The game's main character undergoes development throughout the course of the game and story. I will talk about storytelling and character development in more detail later. Adventure games also include exploration over vast world with the gamer going on quests and solving puzzle along the way. Early adventure games were usually turn-based such as the unforgettable *King's Quest* and *Myst*.

A sub-genre of adventure games is the hybrid Action/Adventure game. This sub-genre is primarily a 3rd person point of view, where the camera shows the avatar. Hit titles such as *God of War*, *Prince of Persia*, and *Soul Reaver* are games that fall into this category just to name a few. These games require exploration as well as destroying enemies with critical timing and technique, thus making them an action as well as adventure game. This sub-genre also integrates a storyline with character development.

Puzzle games are another genre of games. Tetris is a classic example of a puzzle game. Puzzle games are also popular on handheld devices mainly due to their low requirements of processing power and can be played over a short period of time to satisfy the player's "fun fix". Many games include puzzles as mini-games within the main game, usually in adventure or the action/adventure hybrid.

Role-playing games are a sixth genre of games. Role-playing games were introduced with *Dungeons & Dragons*. In this genre there is a storyline, character development, and exploration. Some goals may be to gain experience, seek treasure, and destroy enemies. However, the main focus is on your character or characters and their development. World immersion is essential in this genre as a designer's goal would be to draw the gamer into the fantastic virtual world. *Final Fantasy* is an example of a popular role-playing game. Massively Multiplayer Online Role-Playing Games, or MMORPGs, have emerged due to efficient networks and allow many players to play an RPG online on a large scale. Many MMORPGs have something known as persistent worlds. This means that the game world exists whether you, as a gamer, are logged on or are offline.

The seventh genre of video games is strategy. Strategy games require thought and planning. Strategy games can be real-time or turn-based. Many war games are strategy based as primary goals would be to build an army, plan attacks, and recover and defend. As there are MMORPGs, there are also MMORTS, or Massively Multiplayer Online Real Time Strategy. Sports is another genre as well as Simulations. I will discuss simulation games in further detail later.

Industry Structure and the Development Team

In the gaming industry, there are three primary types of players. The first is the game developer. The second is the publisher. The third is the hardware manufacturer. Taking *Dead or Alive 4* as an example, the hardware manufacturer is Microsoft (Xbox 360), the developer is Team Ninja, and the publisher is TECMO. Sometimes the publisher and developer are the same. An example of this is with *Prince of Persia: The Sands of Time*. The publisher and developer are both Ubisoft.

There exists a relationship between each industry player. The publisher will finance the game being created by the developer. The hardware manufacturer provides licenses and SDKs for the developer to create games for that system. There are also managerial factors between the publisher and hardware manufacturer.

Within the development team, there are different groups of people with different functions. A development team will have people who deal with management, people dealing with the technical side of development, and people who create art and audio assets.

Sometimes other players are involved such as a third party company that does motion capture. A motion capture studio can be expensive and therefore not all developers have them. It is also important to know what motion capture is based on. Motion capture can be done in two different ways. The first is using sensors on actors, while the second is using cameras. A good example for using motion capture may be a quarterback throwing a football, or having a martial artist performing different attack moves for a fighting game. Still, other people who may be involved in development may be a group of people whom worked is outsourced to for the sake of cost. There also may be a legal team to deal with issues such as licensing Marvel superheroes so he or she can be used in a game.

If we break the development team down further, you will find audio engineers and musicians who create background music and sound effects such as explosions, voice-over, and environmental sounds. There will also be user interface designers who design game elements such as a heads up display and the control mechanism. There are also artists and animators. Artists can be divided into two groups. One group is responsible for 2D graphics used for things such as texture mapping or a splash screen. A splash screen is the screen you see when the game starts. I will discuss texture mapping in more detail later. The other group would create 3D Models for the level/world, characters, non-playable characters (NPCs), and items such as weapons or potions. 3D Studio Max or Maya are industry tools to create 3D Models. The animators bring the models to life by giving them motion. A common type of animation is key frame animation. This is where there are many frames and for each *key* frame the model is in a different position, thus when played quickly, gives the illusion of movement. It is also important to know that the positions between key frames, though not specifically set, are interpolated which makes the movement look smooth and not choppy.

There are different types of programmers on the development team. There are AI (Artificial Intelligence) programmers, many times scripting in a language called Lua. There are audio programmers using SDKs such as OpenAL or DirectSound. If there is an online component to the game, there would be network programmers. Network programming is based on socket programming. A socket is something that represents an IP address and port in code. The network programmer would need to decide whether to use TCP or UDP, where TCP is connection oriented and reliable as oppose to UDP which is connectionless but faster and unreliable. The network programmers may develop for a client/server model, or peer to peer. There are also tools programmers that develop tools for other developers and designers to use. Graphics programmers are involved with 3D modeling rendering, animation, lighting and shading of a scene, setting up the camera, and texture mapping. Graphics programmers usually code using OpenGL or Direct3D. I will cover graphics programmer in more detail later. On the development team there are also physics programmers, gameplay programmers, and User Interface programmers.

To make sure there are no errors in the game, the game goes through testing. Thus, you have Quality assurance engineers and play testers. The game will go through alpha testing and beta testing before the final release. The vision person of the game is the lead designer. The producer deals with project management and the publisher finances the game project.

Non-linearity and Interactivity

Games are a unique form of media. They are different from other forms of media, such as literature and film, due to two primary reasons. First, games are non-linear, and second, because of the interactive element.

Books and film are considered linear media where games are non-linear. In linear media, the story starts from the beginning and goes to the end with respect to linear time. A book or movie does not change and there are no variations in the storyline. Furthermore, a book or film is the same every time it is read or viewed. There is an exception with books always being linear. This exception is the "choose your own adventure" books which were non-linear. Quintin Tarantino attempted to create a non-linear form of film, such as Kill Bill or Pulp Fiction, by manipulating scenes with different time frames. However, this was a fake non-linearity as the film was still the same every time it was watched.

Games are by default, truly non-linear. The storyline of a game may look something like this:

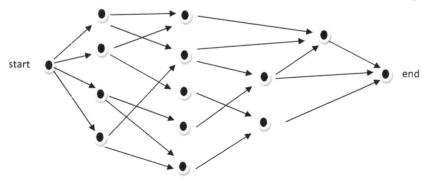

The player has a choice is forming the story of the game. It can also change the next time the game is played. Although, the start and end may be the same, the player can take different paths to reach the same goal. Even, subparts of the game can be reached in more than one way, or even avoided. Furthermore, based on how the game is played, each time the game will be unique no matter how many times it is played. This concept of multiple paths and divergences make the game truly non-linear.

The phenomenon that allows non-linearity is interactivity. The player interacts with the media and therefore changing the outcomes.

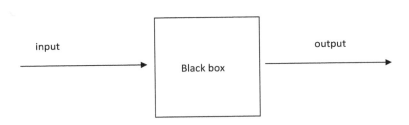

If input = x then output = q

    = y   = r

    = z   = s

For a variable input, there is a variable output.

Interactivity also creates a sense of immersion. Immersion is the idea that makes you feel you are actually "in" the virtual world. The world creates an ambiance and you are the main character in this world. Immersion is created by various game elements such as how the game looks, the sounds, the gameplay and challenges, the avatar, and the interactivity. Creating this sense of world immersion is vital to the gaming experience. Getting "lost" or escaping into this virtual world hooks the gamer to keep playing.

For the interactive input/output system:

1) There must be some form of feedback (ie: auditory, visual, tactile)
2) There can be many forms of output for the same input
3) For no input, there must be no output
4) For valid or invalid input, there must be some indication that it was done

There are other factors involved with interactivity. Interactivity allows self-testing. It also allows exploration of possibilities to reach a goal. With self-testing, the game can have a progression of difficulty. A difficulty curve may look something like this:

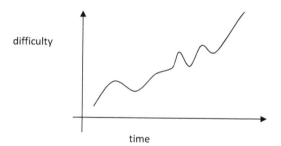

It is important to remember that difficulty curves must be balanced. When you test your abilities and skills, if the game is difficult but doable, then there is satisfaction at success. If it is too difficult, the player will lose interest out of frustration. Thus, the game must be winnable but challenging at the same time. Another example is the Tetris difficulty curve:

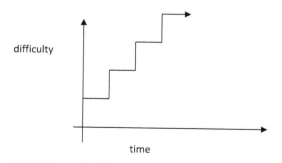

Logic Basics and Flow Charts

Logic Basics

Boolean logic is fundamental and intrinsic in computer hardware as well as software. Boolean operators are used for bitwise operations.

Boolean operators:

AND

OR

NAND

NOR

NOT

XOR

Given:

1 – TRUE

0 – FALSE

AND:

0 AND 0 = 0

0 AND 1 = 0

1 AND 0 = 0

1 AND 1 = 1

OR:

0 OR 0 = 0

0 OR 1 = 1

1 OR 0 = 1

1 OR 1 = 1

NAND:

0 NAND 0 = 1

0 NAND 1 = 1

1 NAND 0 = 1

1 NAND 1 = 0

NOR:

0 NOR 0 = 1

0 NOR 1 = 0

1 NOR 0 = 0

1 NOR 1 = 0

NOT:

NOT 0 = 1

NOT 1 = 0

XOR:

0 XOR 0 = 0

0 XOR 1 = 1

1 XOR 0 = 1

1 XOR 1 = 0

Flow Charts

Flow charts are used to design algorithms that are to be implemented in software. It maps functionality to logical flows. Basically, they are visual representations of certain algorithms or desired functionality. For example, you could use a flow chart to show how a puzzle in a game should work or even a combat system. Therefore, they aid in designing gameplay and game mechanics. Flow charts are created using certain building blocks.

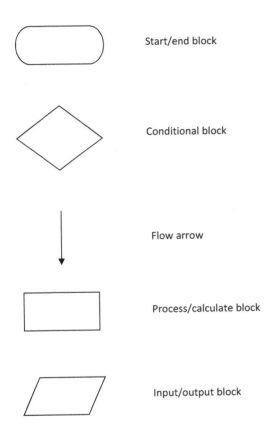

Start/end block

Conditional block

Flow arrow

Process/calculate block

Input/output block

Start/end block:

Use this block for a start state or an end state

Example: Enter level 2

Conditional block:

Use this block when checking for a condition. If the condition is true, choose one flow. If it is false, choose the other flow

Example: Is score greater than 0? If true, go to process block 1. If false, go to process block 2.

Flow arrow:

Shows the direction of flow from one block to another

Example: Go from start block to process block

Process/calculate block:

Use this block when performing changes to variable or other calculations

Example: increment score by 10

Input/Output block:

Use this block when getting input from the user or displaying output to the user

Example: Take input from gamepad

Example Flow Chart:

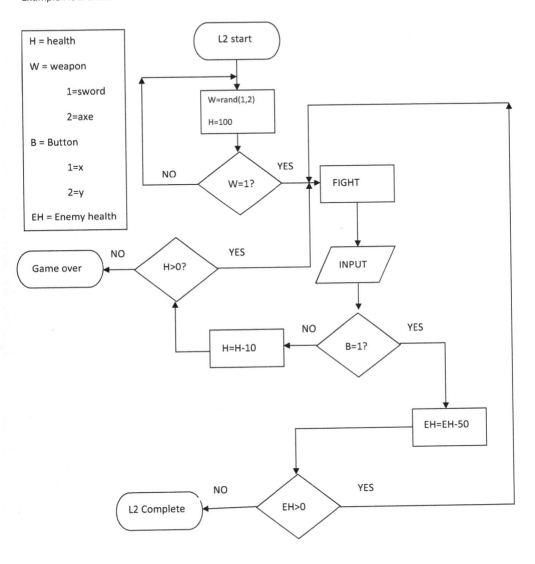

H = health

W = weapon

    1=sword

    2=axe

B = Button

    1=x

    2=y

EH = Enemy health

L2 start

W=rand(1,2)
H=100

W=1?

NO

YES

FIGHT

INPUT

B=1?

NO

YES

H=H-10

EH=EH-50

H>0?

NO

YES

Game over

EH>0

NO

YES

L2 Complete

Design Process

When developing a game, there is a certain flow and structure of the steps taken from when the game is conceived till it's finality and release. In this section, I will cover the phases involved with the development of a game.

Design Process:

1) Concept
2) Pre-production
3) Prototype
4) Production
5) Alpha
6) Beta
7) Gold
8) Post-production

1) Concept

During the concept phase, the idea for the game is decided as well as writing the "one-pager" document. The "one-pager" is a one page summary of the game. It is the selling document of the development team to the publisher. It includes the title of the game and what is known as the high concept. The high concept is one or two sentences describing the game. It should be well thought out, and only in one to two sentences, describe the game holistically. The "one-pager" should reveal the demographics, or target audience for the game as well as features the game will have. Remember, any unique features the game has (no other game has it) should also be briefly discussed. The document should also mention the hardware and software requirements for the game and the target platform. The genre of the game should also be decided during the concept phase.

2) Pre-production

In this phase, the team develops a proposal and undergoes planning for the game. A budget is drawn up for how much the development of the game will cost as well as research for the game. The team is assembled and comes up with the production plan. The production plan elaborates the schedule for development which includes milestones and dates. The Game Design Document (see Appendix A), or GDD, is written during this phase. The GDD encompasses everything that will be in the game. Also, the technical design document (see Appendix B), or TDD, is written. The TDD will aid the programmers when coding.

3) Prototype

Prototyping is the third phase. During this phase, an implementation is developed that portrays the game vision and gameplay. There are two types of prototypes. One type is an analogue prototype. This is a physical representation of the game. The other is a digital prototype that is done in software. The prototype, whether physical or digital, will be presented to the publisher, who finances the project, to see if the game can go into production. In the prototype, unique gameplay features and mechanics should be included. It should also encapsulate the "feel" of the game.

4) Production

If the prototype is approved by the publisher, the game enters the production phase. This is the longest phase and where development of the game takes place. Production time can vary between six months to two years (estimate). The end result of the production phase is a completed game. Therefore, design has been completed, along with programming and art and audio assets. During this phase, the producer must make sure the game is within the budget and on time for the release date.

5) Alpha

Before this phase begins, there should be a completed playable game. This is where "polishing" of the game should occur and "would-like-to-have" features for the game may be dropped to meet the release date. Also, the game manual should be completed in this phase. However, most importantly, this is where rigorous testing of the game occurs. Play-testers are brought in to play the game from start to finish and check for bugs. The bug reports created go back to the programmers for revision of the code. Testing also includes checking for platform compatibility and making sure the software and hardware requirements are met.

6) Beta

During beta, more testing is done. This is where corrected bugs are checked from Alpha and bugs not caught in Alpha are eliminated. Performance tuning also occurs for optimal functionality. The master game media, usually in disc form, is created after the code is finalized and corrected.

7) Gold

Gold is the second last stage of the design process. Here, the master game media goes to be manufactured, and the game is released and distributed.

8) Post-Production

This is the final phase. During post-production, if any problems were discovered after release, patches are created to resolve them. Also, there may be upgrades and/or expansions. Patches are usually free, and upgrades and expansions may be free also. Before this phase, and prior to release, the game should have been marketed.

Chapter 2: Game Design II

Storytelling and Character Development

Stories consist of five primary components; backstory, plot, setting, characters, and theme. The setting is depicted by where and when the story takes place. Some questions a storytelling may ask are what is the political basis when and where the story takes place, where does it take place geographically, and what are the societal rules? Within a setting, there may be a sub-setting, and a sub-sub-setting. These concepts play key roles in level design and enhancing the immersive experience for the gamer. Always remember that the microscopic version of the world should always maintain consistency with the macroscopic view.

The plot of the story usually is constructed in three acts. In act 1, an establishment is made with introducing the characters and revealing the setting. There is also an inciting incident that initiates the events of the story. Toward the end of the first act the main character undergoes a turning point that further drives the story. In act 2, the fundamental journey begins (caused by the turning point in act 1). The character faces various challenges on this journey. The character, during this act, also undergoes another critical change. This is some sort of "bad action" caused by the likeness of a tragic flaw. As a result, the character must face the consequences of this bad action and face more challenges. During the final act, the character has a "moment of truth" and comes to some realization. More challenges present themselves till the point of the ultimate battle, our famous boss fight!

The backstory is simply what happened before the game starts from a story perspective. Many times a backstory is revealed with an introduction clip. The theme is what the story is about and what the message of the story is. The tone of the theme should resonate with everything that happens in the game. In games, it is very important to "show" the story, and simply not "tell" it. This method is called dramatization. Much can be shown during gameplay, but other methods, such as cut-scenes, can also drive the story.

The three act plot:

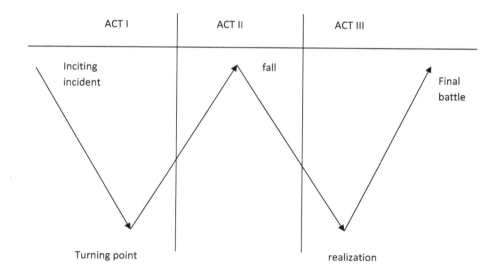

So the question is, why are we attracted to stories? Based on psychological analysis, we are immersed in the story of the virtual world for a few reasons. We attach ourselves to the identity of the main character. We do this because we like to think of ourselves as important figures and want to play the role of a hero, where the ego plays a part. We feel we struggle and want a prize at the end with possible self-appeasement, making our natures almost Machiavellian where the ends justify the means. This makes us more than ordinary and unique giving ourselves a place and potentially understanding the self better. In the end, it is only our self that we can know best.

Some elements that can be used for storytelling are interactivity, which allows the player to direct the storyline, realism and world immersion, which makes the story compelling, and non-linearity, which allows the story to take different paths depending on the choices the player makes in the game. A designer wants to create a moment to moment experience so that the player does not lose interest. However, not all games have stories. The genre of the game will dictate whether a story is required or important. Puzzle games, like Tetris, for example, do not usually have stories.

Character development plays a critical role in games that have a storyline. Most of the time, the player needs familiarity and with the character and needs to be drawn to him or her, which means that the main character is usually not a villain.

The main character undergoes growth throughout the game. The changes in the character are internal changes where at the end of the story, he or she ends up being a leader and great hero. Take, for example, Paul Atredis from Frank Herbert's sci-fi novel, DUNE. The story starts with Paul as a young boy and as the story progresses becomes a tribe leader, then the Madhi, then the Emperor of the Universe by the end of the novel. Paul has undergone drastic development to reach an ultimate goal.

The description of a character is a combination of personality, physicality, and psychology. As a designer, it is important not to tell everything about the character all at once. Also, going back to storytelling, show the changes in the character instead of simply telling them over the course of the game. Another great example of character development is Raistlin, from the DragonLance Chronicles. The mage starts out with Red Robes of neutrality, then changes to where Black Robes of darkness, till finally becomes a god. The admiration for this character comes in when he sacrifices himself from godhood to eternal damnation for the sake of others. This self-sacrifice is the nobility that draws the reader to the character and makes him memorable.

The main character is someone who has mastered his/her struggles where in-game achievement can be seen as a metaphor for internal growth and internal victory. Many challenges are related to what problems we face as individuals or as a society. The progression follows is how we overcome those problems. The one controlled character of the game is known as an avatar and there is a direct link and connection between the player and the avatar.

There are various character types that exist in games. One type is Animals, such as Sonic the Hedgehog or Donkey Kong. Another type of character is fantasy characters such as Lara Croft or Mario. There are also licensed characters such as James Bond or Neo from the Matrix. Mythical characters are common also taken from Greek or Egyptian Mythology. God of War is a prime example for using such characters.

Vital characters in a game fall into different categories. You have the standard good and evil, where there is a Protagonist, which is usually the avatar, and an antagonist. The antagonist is also called the Shadow and is the opposite of the protagonist. The protagonist, or Hero, sometimes has a Mentor, or guide. There are also Allies who help the hero in his or her quest. Finally, another category for a character is a Trickster. The trickster has a neutral role, but tries to hinder the hero from achieving his or her goal.

The avatar's development is a process of self-realization, or self-actualization. This process flows from the micro level to the macro level, starting with the self and expanding to the external. Again, with character development, show the process and dramatize it rather than simply tell or narrate it. One way this is done is via aesthetics. The avatar should be visually appealing determined by the gear, clothes, and physical appearance. Another way the avatar can be visually represented is by movement. Some avatars have signature move, such as Dante's taunt from Devil May Cry.

Interface Design

The interface is the connection between the player and the game. One type of user interface is the graphical user interface, or GUI. The interface must always be designed so that it is player-centric. Therefore, when design the UI, think of yourself as the player. It should be functional and clear. Without an interface a game would be unplayable.

An interface allows actions and provides information. This is information that you cannot directly get from the player or the environment. For example, the interface can show the player's health, points, and weapons inventory. By allowing actions, the interface is allowing gameplay. The interface should also maintain consistency with the story and therefore aid in the immersion. Furthermore, it should reflect information about the character.

Audio is part of an interface. Audio can also provide information. For example, certain sounds are played when certain weapons are selected. If you press an incorrect button, there can be audio feedback that there was an error. Sounds played when weapons are fired is just as relevant as displaying the player's health.

The two main components of an interface are input devices and visual representations. For the visual aspect, the heads up display plays a large role. This can be status, score, health, time, or a mini-map. These are considered passive elements because there is no interaction with them. A main menu screen can have elements such as starting a new game, saving a game, modify settings, or customizing a character. These are considered active elements because there is interaction with them. The display is also part of the interface. This can include something as simple as a monitor or TV and can be even be 360 degree displays or holographic displays. As for input devices, this can be hardware such as a keyboard, mouse, gamepad, joystick, or a USB guitar controller. In arcades, there is more of a variety of input devices such as a car seat with a steering wheel, race pedals, and a shifter, for racing games, or a sniper rifle.

When designing a visual interface, functionality should always come before aesthetics. If a visual interface is very fancy, but difficult to use, then it probably is not a very good design. As for the hardware side of the interface, design or map the controls for input and output as efficiently and naturally as possible.

Game Balancing

The balance of a game is of the utmost important. It should not be too difficult and not too easy either. The game should be consistent, fair, and fun. A person who has more skill should do better than one who has less. A game that consistent challenges means that the game should increase in difficulty by the correct amount at different intervals. A fair game means that if mistakes are made, the player should be given chances to correct the situation. Many games allow the player to choose difficulty levels. This is a good feature to have since by choosing the difficulty level, the player is making the game more fun for himself/herself.

One type of balance is that the balance exists before the game begins and therefore not dynamic. This is called static balance. An example of static balance is giving all the players the same initial conditions and abilities at the start of the game. So this means that, for example, player 1's strength is the same as player 2's strength and the same as player 3's strength at the beginning of the game. This is known as symmetry. As the game progresses, a player can increase their "level" starting from level 1 to level 2 to level 3. This creates a hierarchy of "levels" for all the players. The player goes from one level to the next depending how he or she plays the game. This is known as transitive symmetry and is a linear progression. Intransitive symmetry is circular rather than linear. Rock, paper, scissors is an example of intransitive symmetry. Trade off can be made such as player 1 has 100 health and 50 damage, player 2 has 120 health and 40 damage, and player 3 has 90 health and 60 damage. This is still balanced.

Level Design

When designing a level, the first thing you should do is sketch the layout for the level. For example:

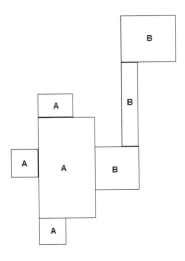

In this example, the player must complete "A" before moving on to "B". Heightfields should also be created. A heightfield is a top view of the level where colors indicate elevation. In grayscale, light shades indicate higher elevation and darker shades indicate lower elevation. For example:

After this, the actual levels are created with a level editor and 3D modeling software. Some features of a level editor are providing different points of view or angles of the level, allowing geometry to be modified, allow navigation through the level, and incorporate scripting. The scripting allows testing of the level as it is being made.

The purpose of the level should primarily enhance gameplay. Each level should also have a primary focus, and the entire level should be designed around that main focus. For orientation purposes, a level should have landmarks. This makes is easier for the player to navigate through the level and determine where he or she is. Also, as a level designer, you should determine which parts of the level are non-linear or linear which should be consistent with the storyline.

There are five main components that a designer should keep in mind when creating the level. The first is the goal of the level. The objective should be conveyed to the player and can be done so with methods such as dialogue, text, or a cut-scene. The second component is the flow of the level. The player should be guided through the level. Also, the player should only be allowed to progress to a certain part of the level is a previous part is completed or completely explored. The designer should also determine how long the level should take to complete. The fourth component is to determine what parts of the level should be accessible at the start and what parts should be accessible as the player progresses. Finally, the levels should maintain consistency with each other from a story perspective and also from a "look and feel" point of view.

As the level progresses, the difficulty level should also increase or adjust itself accordingly. You want to give the player a sense of accomplishment when overcoming a difficult part of the level but not making it unbeatable at the same time. Therefore, there should be high points of difficulty to challenge the player and low points to give the player a break. Both of these may increase overall in a systematic way.

There are also different usages of space in a level. The level exists in 3-space and is a virtual physical environment. The camera is the perspective of the level. The level can be viewed in first person, top down, isometric, side view, or 3rd person behind the avatar. These perspectives depend on where the camera is placed. The second usage of space in a level is the scale of the environment and objects in the world. The sizes of the objects are relative where a designer may want to make important objects larger and not as important ones smaller. The size of the avatar itself partially determines the "look and feel". The larger the avatar, the more detail is required since the player is seeing the avatar all the time. A smaller avatar is usually used by the camera zooming so that more of the world is encompassed in its view. Games that involve more exploring may have a zoomed out camera. Determining the terrain type also adds to the "look and feel" and should match the storyline. With terrain, a choice needs to be made about its level of detail, or LOD. There are algorithms that can be used for terrain dynamic LOD which changes the amount of polygons used in different areas at different times, usually depending on where the camera is. The terrain is also texture mapped. Examples of terrain textures are grass, stone, or dirt. Finally, setting the boundaries can be a tricky, but important element. Since the world cannot be infinite, boundaries are necessary. Some objects that can be used as boundaries are trees, mountains, or water. Invisible boundaries are never good and reflect bad design.

Gameplay

Gameplay is the choices, challenges, and consequences that a player makes and faces in a game. The gameplay should be intertwined with the plot and each should reinforce the other. The structure of gameplay is based on a rule system. For example, if the player does "x", then "y" will happen. The "x" is the choice the player has made to overcome challenge "a", and the result is "y".

Gameplay incorporates winning and losing conditions. So, the question to every game, is "how do you win?". This may be by defeating a final boss non-player character, winning a race, having the high score, or conquering a world. If there is a way to win, then there is also a way to lose. One way of losing may be to run out of health.

Going back to defeating a boss as a winning condition, means that you win while the boss loses. So you gain +1 for winning and the boss gets -1 for losing. The sum of these two is 0 and is called a zero-sum game where there is one winner and one loser. This can also apply to a two player game, such as a fighting game. As oppose to a zero-sum game, there is also a non-zero sum game where the players do not have completely opposing interests.

There are different types of challenges that a game can have. Killing enemies in a 3rd person action adventure, or a first person shooter, is just one type. A single game can, and usually does, incorporate different types of challenges. For example, in a 3rd person action adventure, aside from killing enemies, there may be puzzle solving and exploration as other challenges.

Some of the other types of challenges are puzzle solving, exploration and navigation, mini-games, and resource management. Puzzle solving is a type of challenge that exists in Tetris. Part of the challenge in Tomb Raider is exploration and figuring out where to go. Also, many games incorporate resource management. For example, in Quake, you know that you need to have full health to defeat a certain Strogg, and therefore find a medkit first. Or, to defeat another Strogg, you need a nail gun so you switch weapons.

The Dot and Cross Product

Recall vectors from chapter 1. There are two fundamental vector operations that exist in computer graphics and therefore video games. The first is the dot product. This is a scalar operation that is used to find the angle between two vectors. If the dot product is 0, then the vectors are perpendicular to each other.

$$\text{Let } V_1 = B_{point} - A_{point}$$

$$\text{Let } V_2 = C_{point} - A_{point}$$

$$V_1 \bullet V_2 = x_1x_2 + y_1y_2 + z_1z_2$$

Or

$$V_1 \bullet V_2 = |V_1||V_2|\cos\theta$$

$$\theta = \arccos((V_1 \bullet V_2)/(|V_1||V_2|))$$

where θ is the angle between the vectors

The cross product is used to determine the vector that is perpendicular to two given vectors. A surface normal is determined by the cross product.

$$V1 \times V2 = \det \begin{bmatrix} i & j & k \\ a1 & a2 & a3 \\ b1 & b2 & b3 \end{bmatrix}$$

$$= i(a2b3) + j(a3b1) + k(a1b2) - i(a3b2) - j(a1b3) - k(a2b1)$$

$$= ((a2b3 - a3b2), (a3b1 - a1b3), (a1b2 - a2b1))$$

This result is the vector perpendicular to the original vectors.

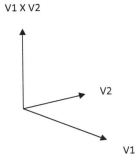

V1 X V2

V2

V1

A Core Development Team

Management:

Producer

Design:

Lead Designer (vision person)

UI designers

Level designers

Programming:

Lead

Audio

Network

Artificial Intelligence

Tools

Gameplay

Graphics

Physics

Art:

Lead

3D Modelers

2D Artists

Animators

FX

Audio:

Sound effects

Background music

Voice-over actors

Chapter 3: Introduction to Programming in C++

C++ is the most commonly used programming language for video games. This is because it is efficient and fast. Most game engines also are developed with C++. In this chapter, we will discuss procedural programming in C++ and move on to object oriented programming in the next chapter.

Introduction Example

```
#include <iostream>

using namespace std;

int main(){

        char x;

        cin>>x;

        cout<< "Hello World!"<<endl;

        return 0;

}
//brief summary
//iostream - input/output library
//char - data type
//x - variable
//cin>> - take input from console
```

//cout<< - output to console

//"Hello World!" - string to output to console

//endl - new line

//; - end statement

// are comments and not part of compiled code

Data Types and Variables

A variable is a representation of a memory location that holds some data. The data at this memory location can be changed, and hence the term variable. The memory location is on the stack, which occurs during compilation of the code. So using the variable is using the data stored at that memory location. For example, you can have a variable *x*, and assign it the value of 5, which can be changed later in the program to 10. Behind the scenes, the program will go to the memory where *x* is allocated and see the value at that location, which in this example was first 5, then 10.

There is a convention to what the variable can be named. The conditions are:

1) Must begin with a letter
2) Can include only letters, numbers, or underscore (no punctuation)
3) The max characters that can be used is 32
4) It cannot be a C++ keyword
5) The variable name is case sensitive

There are different types of data that a variable can hold. The different data types are:

1) *char*

This is one ascii character and is one byte in size in memory. So a variable can be declared as type *char* and store one ascii character. For example:

char firstInitial = 'F';

char is the data type
firstInitial is the variable name
= is the assignment operator (store F in firstInitial)
F is the literal and must be encompassed by single quotes
; represents the end of the statement

2) *short*

A *short* is a size of two bytes in memory and is an integer value. The values that a *short* data type variable can hold are -32,768 to 32,767. If you use the keyword *unsigned* before *short* then this means only use positive values and the range changes to 0 to 65,535. Examples are:

short myNum = 1345;

unsigned short myNum2 = 33000;

3) *integer*

An *integer* is a 32 bit value. So this means that the values range from -2,147,483,648 to 2,147,483,647. However, an *int* can also be *unsigned*. Some examples of declaring and assigning a value of 15 to an *int* variable are:

int x;

x=15;

or

int x = 15;

or

int x = 0;

x=15;

The first example is declaring x and then assigning it a value of 15. This method initially gives x garbage data when declared. The second declares and assigns at the same time. The third, declares and initializes x to 0, and then assigns it a value of 15.

4) *float*

A *float* is a decimal value of four bytes and seven digits of precision.

5) *double*

A *double* is a decimal value of eight bytes with fifteen digits of precision. An example is:

double y = 3.45;

We could have had this value stored in a *float* as well:

float y2 = (float)3.45;

This example uses something known as type casting. We will talk more about this later. Basically, the value 3.45 is interpreted as a double, so we need to "force" it to be a float. We could have also done:

float y2 = 3.45f;

6) *bool*

A *bool* is one byte of data that can be either true or false. An example is:

bool isCorrect = false;
//do something
isCorrect = true;

cin, cout, and const

cin takes input from the console and cout output to the console. For example the code:

int x=0;

cin>>x;

cout<<"You have entered: "<<x<<endl;

will place the value you entered in the console window in *x* (as long as it is an integer) and the cout statement will output the value to the console window.

A keyword in C++ is *const*. This is used when declaring a variable. If a variable is declared as *const* , then that value for the variable cannot be changed. If you try to change it, the compiler will throw an error. An example is:

const double pi = 3.14;

now the value of pi cannot be changed.

An example of what will cause an error is:

const int y = 415;

y=417; // ERROR

This means that the value of the variable must be set/assigned when the variable is declared. So, this would be incorrect since declaring without initializing places junk data in the variable when it is declared:

const int z;

z=109; //ERROR

Type Conversions and Casting

Type conversion and casting is used to change the data type of data. One type of conversion is implicit type conversion. This is where the compiler changes the data type as needed. This can mean either a promotion or demotion and the compiler will see the data type of a memory location and act as required. An example of promotion is:

double x=0;

int y=10;

x=y; //Promotion

So, the conversion occurs from the "smaller" data type (int) to "larger" (double). Therefore, the value of x will end up having decimal places due to the conversion and promotion. Demotion converts the data from a "larger" data type to "smaller". An example would be:

double x = 45.6

int y = 0;

y = x; //Demotion

Since the double has been demoted to an int, the resulting value of y will not have decimal places as they are dropped and the final value of y would be 45.

During arithmetic operations (more on this later), such as x + y, and the data types do not match, the variable of the "lower" data type is always promoted to the "higher" data type. For example:

int x=5;

double y=6.1;

double z=0;

z = x + y; //x get promoted to 5.0(double) and z becomes 11.1

Another example is:

int x=5;

double y = 6.1;

int z=0;

z = x + y; //z is 11

What happened here was that first, x was promoted, and then the result of x+y is demoted and stored in z, since z is an int.

Explicit type conversion is when you explicitly convert from one data type to another. For example:

float a = (float) 323.3;

//323.3 is a double that gets forced to be a float and stored in a float variable

Another example is:

double x = 0;

int y = 5;

x = (double)y; //y is forced to be a doube, thus with decimal places and stored in the double variable x

if you had:

double finalValue;

int x = 3;

int y = 2;

finalValue = x/y;

You would expect to get 1.500... but instead get 1.000.... This is because x/y is still an integer and the decimal places are dropped off and then promoted to a double data type. To get the correct value, you need to type cast.

finalValue = (double)x/y;

//x is forced to be a double, y get promoted to a double and stored as 1.500...

Arithmetic Operators

Operator	Description	Precedence
=	assignment	
( )	Override other precedence rules	1
-	Negation	2
*	Multiply	3
/	Divide	3
%	Modulas	3
+	Add	4
-	Subtract	4

So based on this, if you had:

int x;

x = ((14*5)+1)*3;

x would be 213.

Other operators are:

Operator	Description	example
++(postfix)	Increment by 1 after	i++; //i = i+1;
--(postfix)	Decrement by 1 after	i--; //i = i-1;
++(prefix)	Increment by 1 before	++i;
--(prefix)	Decrement by 1 before	--i;
-=	Subtract from current value and assign	i-=100; //i = i -100;
+=	Add to current value and assign	i+=100; // i = i+100;
*=	Multiply by value and assign	i*=100; //i=i*100;
/=	Divide by value and assign	i/=100; //i = i/100;

Boolean Operators

Boolean operators are used in conditional statements. For example you could check if a certain condition is true or false and then act accordingly. You are comparing the left hand side value/variable of the operator to the right hand side value/variable of the operator. So, one Boolean operator is: ==

LHS == RHS

If the LHS is equal to the RHS then this statement is true, else it is false.

Some example are:

1==1	true
1==2	false
true==true	true
false==true	false

```
bool x = true;
bool y = false;
```

x==y	false

```
double q=2.0;
double r=2.1;
```

q==r	false

```
char c='A';
char t;
t=c; //assignment
```

t==c	true

LHS > RHS

Check if the LHS is greater than the RHS. An example is:

```
int x = 2;
int y = 3;
```

x>y   false

y>x   true

LHS >= RHS

Check if the LSH is greater than or equal to the RHS. An example is:

int x = 2;

int y = 3;

x>=y   false

y>=x   true

if y = 2, then:

x>=y   true

LHS < RHS

Check if the LHS is less than the RHS.

LHS <= RHS

Check if the LHS is less than or equal to the RHS

LHS != RHS

Check if the LHS is not equal to the RHS. For example:

bool q = true;

bool r = true;

q!=r   false

int x = 1;

int y = 2;

x!=y   true

!

This is the negation operator. So if the value is true, then the result is false, and if it is false, the result is true. For example:

!true   false

!false   true

LHS && RHS

This is the Boolean AND operation discussed in chapter 1. The truth table again is (given 0 is false and 1 is true):

0 && 0   false

0 && 1   false

1 && 0   false

1 && 1   true

Expression can also be used.

Expression1 && Expression2 where Expression1 and Expression2 results in a true or false value. For example:

int x = 2;

int y = 2;

double z = 1.1;

double w = 2.1;

(x==y)&&(z==w)   false (x==y is true and z==w is false, so the AND of true and false is false)

If w=1.1 then,

(x==y)&&(z==w)   true

More examples:

int x=2;

int y=3;

bool q=true;

bool r=true;

(x<=y)&&(q==r)   true

(x>=y)&&(q==r)   false

(x!=y)&&(q==r)   true

!((x!=y)&&(q==r))   false

!((x!=y)&&(!(q)==r))   true

LHS || RHS

This is the boolean OR operator. The truth table is:

0 || 0   false

0 || 1   true

1 || 0   true

1 || 1   true

Some examples are:

char s = 'C';

char t = 'D';

int x = 1;

int y = 2;

(s==t)||(x<y)   true

Let's say that x = 2 now:

(s==t)||(x<=y)   true

More examples:

int x = 1;

int y = 2;

char c = 'c';

char t = 't';

double q = 2.1;

double r = 2.1;

((q==r)||(c==t))&&(x<=y)   true

((q!=r)||(c!=t))&&(x!=y)   true

int x = 1;

int y = 2;

int z =0;

z = x+y;

(y>=x)||(z>5)   true

(y>=x)&&(z>5)   false

(((x+y)>=z)&&(z<5))   true

(((x+y)>=z)||(z<5))   true

(((x+y)>z)&&(z<5))   false

if Statements

if statement are conditional statements that check whether an expression is true or false. If the expression is true, then some code is executed, and if it is false, that block of code is skipped.

if(expression){

        //execute this code because expression is true

}

//continue here regardless of whether expression is true or false

An example is:

```
int main(){
        int x=1;
        int y=2;
        if(x==y){
                x+=y;
        }
        return 1;
}
```

Some other examples:

```
int main(){
        int x=1;
        int y=2;
        if(x>y){
                y=x;
        }
        x=y;
        return 1;
}
```

```
int main(){
        int x=2;
        int y=3;
        double z=0.0;
```

```
        if(x!=y){

                y++;

                z=2.1;

        }

        z+=1.0;

        return 1;

}

//At the end of code:

//x is 2

//y is 4

//z is 3.1


int main(){

        int x=5;

        int y=6;

        bool z=true;

        if((x<=y)&&(z)){

                //will code here execute?

        }

        //code here will execute regardless whether the check is true or false

}
```

Going along with if statements, there is also an if-else statement. With an if-else, execute some code if the expression is true, or some other code if the expression is false.

```
if(expression){

        //execute only if true
```

```
}
else{
        //execute only if expression is false
}
```

An example is:

```
bool hasArmor=false;
int health=100;
int damage=10;
if(hasArmor){
        health-=damage/2;
}
else{
        health-=damage;
}
```

An extension of the if-else statement is an if-else if statement. With this, check to see if the if statement is true and if it is, execute some code. If it is not, use an else if to check if a different expression is true or false. If it is true, execute some code, and if not continue to the next part of the code. However, only one segment of code can execute. This means that even if the expression from the if, and the expression of the else if are true, only the first if block will execute. The determination of which block to execute if more than one expression is true is in the order of appearance. Also, you can have multiple else if statements after the original if statement. Here is a template:

```
If(expression1){
        //only if expression1 is true
}
else if(expression2){
```

```
            //only if expression2 is true and expression1 is false
}
```

Some examples:

```
int x=5;
if(x>10){
        //no
}
else if(x<3){
        //no
}
else if(x>=4){
        //yes
}


if(x==5){
        //yes
}
else if(x>3){
        //no
}
else if(x<10){
        //no
}
```

Finally, there is an if-else if-else statement. It is just like an if-else if statement, but if none of the previous expressions are true, then the final else will always execute. So:

```cpp
if(expression1){

        //code here

}

else if(expression2){

        //code here

}

else{

        //will only execute if expression1 and expression2 are false

}
```

You can have as many else if statements before the final else and after the initial if.

Loops

There are three types of loops in C++. Loops are used to execute a block of code a certain number of times, and then continuing on. The types of loops are for loops, while loops, and do-while loops. Base your loops on flow charts and always avoid having infinite loops.

The for loop starts at a certain value for iterating and then stops when the iterator reaches a value while it changes value throughout the process. A simple example is:

```cpp
int y=0;

for(int i=0; i<10; i++){

        y++;

}
```

Here, i is the iterator that is initialized to 0. At every iteration, I increments by 1 and the loop continues while i is less than 10. Thus, if we outputted y at each step, we would get, 1,2,3,4,5,6,7,8,9,10. Code that would yield the same results would be:

```
int y=0;

for(int i=0; i<20; i+=2){

        y++;

}
```

Another example is:

```
for(int i=20; i>0; i-=2){

        cout<<i<<endl;

}
```

So a general description would be:

```
for(variable initialization; condition; variable update){

        //execute till condition is false

}
```


Another loop is the while loop. A while loop keeps looping/iterating as long as a certain condition is true. An example is:

```
int x=0;

while(x<10){

        x++;

}
```

In this example, the loop goes through 10 iterations. You can use any type of Boolean expression as a condition for the while loop to continue iterating or ending.

The final type of loop is the do-while loop. This is very similar to the while loop. However, the difference is that with a do-while loop, you are guaranteed that it will execute at least once since there is no "check" in the first iteration.


```
int z=0;
```

```
do{

    z++;

}while(z<10);
```

An important keyword that affects loops is break. If break executes then the program will exit from the loop that the break statement is in regardless of how many loop iterations are left. Usually, you would use break in a conditional statement to check something, and if the condition is true, you call break to break out of the loop. An example is:

```
for(int i=0; i<20; i++){

    cout<<i<<endl;

    if(i==10){

        break;

    }

}
```

So, in this example, as soon as the iterator, i, is equal to 10, the program exits the for loop. Therefore, the loop will go through 10 iterations.

Another important keyword used in loops is continue. When the program sees continue in a loop, the rest of the code in the loop is skipped and goes on to the next iteration. Like break, continue is commonly used in a conditional statement. For example:

```
for(int i=0; i<20; i++){

    if(i=10){

        continue;

    }

    cout<<i<<endl;

}
```

In this example, the output to the console will be: 0,1,2,3,4,5,6,7,8,9,11,12,13,14,15,16,17,18,19. Because of the continue if i is 10, the cout statement is skipped and the loop goes on to the next iteration and therefore 10 is not outputted to the console.

The switch Statement

Another control structure is the switch statement. In a switch statement, you check to see the value of a variable and match it up with certain cases. If the value matches the case, then the code for that case is executed. Break is also commonly used in a switch statement so that when the code for a matched case executes, the program will exit the switch statement due to the break. An example is:

```
char grade = 'B';

switch(grade){

        case 'A':

                cout<<"You got an A"<<endl;

                break;

        case 'B':

                cout<<"You got a B"<<endl;

                break;

        case 'C':

                cout<"You got a C"<<endl;

                break;

        default:

                cout<<"You failed"<<endl;

                break;

}
```

In this example, you will get the output to the console "You got a B", and then the switch exits because of the break. You can have as many cases as you like and you can also check values of different data types like an integer (You will not use single quotes in the cases for integer values). The default case is optional. What it means is that if none of the cases before don't match up, then the code in default will execute. Finally, if more than one case match up, then both will execute given that there is no break after the first case match. If there is a break, then only the first case match will execute and then break out of the switch.

Nested Control Structures

You can nest the various control structure we have discussed already. Here are some examples:

Example 1:

```
int y=0;

int x=10;

bool z=false;

if(x<30){

        y++;

        if(x<=10){

                z=true;

                y++;

        }

}
//results: x=10, y=2, z=true
```


Example 2:

```
int z=0;

bool x=true;

int c=10;

if(x==true){

        z=5;

        if(c>10){

                z++;
```

```
        }
}
else{
        z=7;
        if(c<10){
                z++;
        }
}
//results: c=10, x=true, z=5


Example 3:
//same initial values as example 2
if(x==true){
        z=5;
        if(c>10){
                z++;
        }
        else{
                z+=2;
        }
}
else{
        z=7;
        if(c>10){
                z++;
```

```cpp
        }
    else{
            z+=2;
        }
}
//results:x=true, c=10, z=7
```

Example 4:

```cpp
double score=85;
char grade='B';
if(score>70){
        switch(grade){
                case 'A':
                        cout<<"you got an "<<grade<<endl;
                        break;
                case 'B':
                        cout<<"you got a "<<grade<<endl;
                        break;
                case 'C':
                        cout<<"you got a "<<grade<<endl;
                        break;

                }
}
    else{
```

```
switch(grade){

        case 'D':

                cout<<"you got a "<<grade<<endl;

                break;

        case 'F':

                cout<<"you got an "<<grade<<endl;

                break;

    }

}
//results: You got a B
```

Example 5:

```
int number=0;

for(int i=0; i<5; i++){

        for(int j=0; j<5; j++){

                number=i+j;

                cout<<number<<endl;

        }

}
//output
//0 1 2 3 4 1 2 3 4 5 2 3 4 5 6 3 4 5 6 7 4 5 6 7 8
```

Example 6:

```
bool x=true;

int y=0;
```

```
while(x){

    y++;

    if(y==10){

        x=false;

    }

}
```

Example 7:

```
bool x=true;

int y=0;

do{

    y++;

    if(y==10){

        break;

    }

    else{

        continue;

    }

    y++;

}while(x);

//x never becomes false

//the second y++ never executes
```

Example 8:

```
int y=0;
```

```
int q=0;

for(int i=0; i<20; i++){

        y++;

        q=i%2;

        if(q!=0){

                i+=2;

        }

}
//10 iterations
```

Example 9:

```
int x=5;

int q=25;

bool y=true;

while(y==true){

        bool z=true;

        x+=q;

        while(z){

                q++;

                if(q>30){

                        z=false;

                }

                if(q>35){

                        z=false;

                        y=false;
```

```
            }

        }

}
```
//x will be 195

Functions

A function is a block of code that performs some task. Functions are used for two primary reasons. The first is to avoid rewriting the same code multiple times. Thus, the function is called when needed to perform the same task. The second reason is that it helps break down code into more manageable parts. There are two types of functions. The first is value returning functions and the second is void functions, or functions that do not return a value. The function of utmost important is the main() function. This is the function that executes first when the program is run. It is the entry point for the program. For example, using the main() function, you could have it return an integer or be a void function:

int main(){

    //some code

    return 1; //return success

}

or

void main(){

    //some code

    //no return value

}

Functions have a prototype associated with them. The generalization of the prototype is:

returnType functionName(parameterList);

The returnType can be of any data type and must match what the function returns, with the keyword return. The functionName can be any name that you want it to be that is a valid name. The parameterList can have as many parameters as you like of any data type. The parameters are passed into the function for the function to use for calculation and manipulation when it is called from somewhere else in the program. There may also be no parameters at all. The function name and parameter list make up what is known as the function signature. The signature does not include the return type.

A function consists of three required parts. They are the function prototype, the function definition, and the function call.

Example 1:

#include <iostream>

using namespace std;

int func1(); //prototype, function that returns an integer and takes no parameters

int x;

int y;

int main(){ //program entry point

   int q;

   x=5;

   y=4;

   q=func1();//call the function and store the return value in q

   cout<<q;

   return 1;//return success to main()

}

//function definition

int func1(){

   int z;

   z=x+y;

   return z;

}

The function prototype is usually before main() and the definition is outside of main().

Example 2:

```cpp
#include <iostream> //input and output to the console

using namespace std; //use the standard namespace

int func2(int x, int y); //function prototype, takes two parameters of type integer

int main(){

    int q;

    q=func2(5,4); //call the function with values 5 and 4 as parameters and store return value in q

    cout<<q; //output is 9

    return 1;

}
//function definition
int func2(int x, int y){

    int z;

    z=x+y; //x is 5 and y is 4 (depends on what values are used when the function is called)

    return z;

}
```

Variable Scope

In a program, variables have a certain scope. This can be considered as the lifetime of the variable. There are two types of scope a variable can have; global and local. A global variable can be accessed and used anywhere in the program after it has been declared and the data it holds is maintained.

Example 1:

```cpp
#include <iostream>

using namespace std;
```

```
int x; //global

int y; // global

double z; //global;

int main(){

        //can reference x, y, and z

        return 1;

}

//can use x,y,z in function definition also
```

Variables with local scope have a lifetime only within a block of code that is determined by {}, such as in function definitions or control structures.

Example 2:

```
int main(){

        int x=0; //x is local to the main() function and cannot be accessed and used outside of it

        return 1;

}
```

Example 3:

```
if(someValue>10){

        int y=5; //y is local to the if statement

}
```

Example 4:

```
if(someValue>10){

        int a = 7; //local to if

        if(someOtherValue>5){

                bool check=true; //local to the if (nested, second if)

                a++; //can access a here because second if is inside {} of first if
```

```
        }
}
//cannot access a or check here
```

Example 5:

```
int main(){
        int x=10; //local to main()
        if(x==10){
                int y=5; //local to if
        }
        else{
                int z=3; //local to else
        }
        x=y+z; //ERROR because y and z are out of scope
        return 1;
}
```

Example 6:

```
double func2(bool q); //function prototype with one Boolean parameter using a variable q
int main(){
        double r; //local to main()
        r = func2(true); //call func2 passing in true and storing the return value in r
        cout<<r;
        return 1;
}
double func2(bool s){
        double x; //local to fun2
```

```
if(s==true){

    x=3.33;

    return x; //x is local but it's value is returned to where the function is called from and
    //stored in r

}

else{

    x=4.25;

    return x;

}

}
```

Function Parameters

It is important to note that when you create a function prototype where the function has parameters, the variables used can be any valid variable name. The important thing is the data type. Therefore, when creating a function definition, the names of the variables used are not important (as long as they are valid variable names), and can be different variable names as long as the number of parameters match, along with the data types. Furthermore, the program knows to use a particular function definition when a function is called by the signature of the function. So, if you had a function called reduceHealth that had an integer and a Boolean as parameters, the program knows to use the definition for reduceHealth because its name is used and values of an integer and Boolean are passed in when it is called.

It is not necessary to use actual values as parameters when calling a function. You can pass variables that hold data to a function when it is called as long as they are of the correct data type. For example, the following calls to the same function do the same thing:

void func3(int x, int y); //function prototype

//...some code

int a = 3;

int b = 7;

func3(a,b); //function call

func3(3, 7); //function call

As mentioned before, having functions avoid the need for rewriting the same block if code. You can see this in the following example:

double calcArea(int radius);

int main(){

      double area;

      int radius;

      cout<<"Enter radius: "<<endl;

      cin>>radius;

      area = calcArea(radius);

      cout<<area<<endl;

      cout<<"Enter new radius:"<<endl;

      cin>>radius;

      area = calcArea(radius);

      cout<<area<<endl;

      return 1;

}

double calcArea(int radius){

      double area;

      area = radius*radius*3.14;

      return area;

}

What we have seen so far when using functions is a call by value method. Functions can pass in parameters as call by value or call by reference. With call by value, copies of the parameters are made when the function is called. This means that when the function is called, because copies of the parameters are made, if the function makes changes to the parameters in its definition, the changes are made only to the copies and not the original parameters that are passed in when the function is called. For example:

```
void callByValFunc(int x);

int main(){

        int testVar=4;

        callByValFunc(testVar); //copy of testVar is used

        cout<<testVar<<endl; //outputs 4 even though the function made a change to the parameter

        return 1;

}

void callByValFunc(int x){ //when this function is called, x is a copy of testVar

        x+=5; //x is 9

        //void function so no return value

}
```

The copy of testVar is deleted from memory as soon as the function completes. To actually make changes to the parameter that is passed in, you need to call the function using call by reference. If this is done, the function works at the same memory address of the parameter, thus being able to modify it and maintain its updated value (if it is actually changed). This is opposed to working only with a copy of the parameter as call by reference works with the actual original parameter. To call by reference, the function needs to use the & operator before the variable name itself in the function prototype and in the function definition. It is not required when the function is called.

Example 1:

```
void foo(int &x);

int main(){

        int num = 27;

        foo(num);

        cout<<num<<endl; //num is 59, not 27

        return 1;
```

```
}
void foo(int &x){

        x = x+32; // x is at the same memory address as num when the function is called, so if x is
        //changed, num is changed

}
```

If the ampersand was not used, and the functioned was called by call by value, x and num would be at different memory addresses so changing one, would not change the other. However, the data held at num would be copied over to the memory location of x.

You can also change the values of more than one parameter when calling by reference. For example:

```
bool foo2(int &x,double &y);

int main(){

        int q=5;

        double r = 2.21;

        if(foo2(q,r)){

                q+=3;

                r+=1.1;

        }

        else{

                q+=4; //q is 11

                r+=2.2; //r is 4.5

        }

        return 1;

}
bool foo2(int &x, double &y){

        x+=2;

        y+=0.09;
```

```
if(x>10){

        return true;

}

else{

        return false;

}

}
```

pow() and rand()

Two common functions are pow() and rand(). pow() is used to raise a number to a specified power. rand() is a random number generator. To use pow(), you need to include math.h (we will talk about include files later). The function takes two parameters. The first parameter is the base, and the second is the exponent. So, saying pow(x,y), raises x to the y power. In mathematics notation, this would be: x^y. The return value of pow() is the result of raising the first parameter to the second. The return value and both parameters are of a double data type.

rand() is a random number generator. It does not take any parameters and returns a random integer in the range of 0 to RAND_MAX. RAND_MAX can vary but is at least 32767. However, there is a way where you can obtain a random number within a different range. To do this, you need to use the modulas (%) operator. So saying, rand() % 100, will return a random value between 0 and 99. The formula used to obtain a value within a certain range is: lowerBound + rand() % ((upperBound-lowerBound)+1). So if you wanted a random number between 50 and 100, 50 would be your lowerBound and 100 your upperBound which makes the equation: int x = 50 + rand()%((100-50)+1).

Arrays

An array is a structure that can hold more than one value of a certain data type. An array can hold data of any data type. This means an array can hold values of data types of bool, int, char, double, float, etc. Here is an example of a declaration of an array that holds ten integers:

int myArray[10];

int is the type of data the array holds, myArray is the name of the array, and the 10 in square brackets is the number of elements that are in the array. The name of an array can be any valid variable name. Other examples are:

double myArray2[5];//array that holds 5 double values

char myArray3[20];//array that holds 20 char values

bool myArray4[7];//array that holds 7 boolean values

This is simply declaring the array and the elements of the array do not hold any meaningful values. After declaring, the programmer needs to assign values to each element of the array. This can be done in various ways. One way is to declare the array and have values assigned at the same time. The way this is done is as follows:

int newArray[5] = {1,2,3,4,5};

In this case 1 is in the first element of the array, 2 in the second, 3 in the third, and so on.

It is also possible to initialize the array with values without specifying the length/size of the array. In this case, you would omit placing a value in the square brackets as such:

int newArray2[] = {1,2,3,4,5};

The compiler determines the size of the array by the number of values used in the curly braces.

Also, we can assign a value to a specific element of an array and use it or access it by indexing it. When you are indexing an array, the index to use for the first element of the array is always 0. So if an array had 10 elements, the values to index that array is 0 through 9. An representation of this is:

Element	1	2	3	4	5	6	7	8	9	10
index	0	1	2	3	4	5	6	7	8	9

If you had an integer array of 5 elements, then declaring and assigning values to the elements would be as follows:

int num[5]; //declaring and integer array of five elements

num[0] = 23;

num[1] = 15;

num[2] = 10;

num[3] = 57;

num[4] = 2001;

We can then access values of this array by indexing. For example:

if(num[2] >=10){

       //some code

}

Or, if we wanted to store the value of an element of the array in another variable, we could:

int val;

val = num[4];

cout<<val; //output would be 2001

If you try to index the array with an index not the range of the size of the array you will get an error. For example:

num[5] = 22; //ERROR. Only 5 elements in the array, not 6

You can also assign different values to the various elements of the array throughout the code as long as the data types match and you are indexing within the size of the array.

When you declare an array without initializing it, the elements of the array holds "junk" data. Therefore, it is always good practice to make sure you initialize the array after declaring it and before assigning it other values later in the program.

int test[10];

for(int i=0; i<10; i++){

       test[i] = 0; //initialize all elements with 0

}

double x=1.1;

double x2[20];

for(int j=0; j<20; j++){

```
        x2[j] = x;

        x+=0.1;

}
```

As mentioned before, the values of the elements of the array can be modified anywhere in the code after the array has been declared. So:

char myWord[4];

myWord[0] = 'c';

myWord[1] = 'a';

myWord[2] = 'r';

myWord[3] = '\0';//null character

//...some code

myWord[2] = 't';

cout<<myWord; //output is cat

The arrays we have seen so far are 1-dimensional arrays. 2-dimensional arrays can also be created. With 2D arrays you have multiple rows and multiple columns as part of the data structure. An example of declaring a 2D array would be:

int arr[5][5];

This array holds only integer values, it's name is arr, and it have 5 elements in the first dimension and 5 elements in the second dimension. When you want to access/assign a certain value from/to the array, you would index it with an index for the first dimension as well as the second dimension. So for the 5 X 5 2D array, it holds 25 values/elements.

[0][0]	[0][1]	[0][2]	[0][3]	[0][4]
[1][0]	[1][1]	[1][2]	[1][3]	[1][4]
[2][0]	[2][1]	[2][2]	[2][3]	[2][4]
[3][0]	[3][1]	[3][2]	[3][3]	[3][4]
[4][0]	[4][1]	[4][2]	[4][3]	[4][4]

We can use for loops to assign values for each element in the array as currently, with just declaring the array and specifying the size, it does not hold any meaningful data.

```
for(int i=0; i<5; i++){
        for(int j=0; j<5; j++){
                arr[i][j] = i+j;
        }
}
```

After this, the 2D array's values would be:

0	1	2	3	4
1	2	3	4	5
2	3	4	5	6
3	4	5	6	7
4	5	6	7	8

Vector

The vector class is part of the standard template library (STL). We saw that an array is of a fixed size that cannot change by either increasing or decreasing in the number of elements it has. So, what do we do if we want a data structure that we can add or delete elements, making it dynamic? The answer is to use the vector. It is just like an array, but can change size. To use the vector data structure, you need to include the vector header file (more on including header files later).

#include <vector>

To declare a vector, you specify you are using the vector class, the type of data the vector can hold, and the name of the vector that is a valid variable name. An example is:

vector<int> myVector;

//vector is the keyword

//int specifies the type of data the vector will hold

//myVector is the name we have given to the vector

(Note, we did not specify the size of the vector)

We can index the vector just like and array.

```
if(myVector[0]==25){

//some code

}
```

But before we can use the vector in this way, we need to add values and elements to it. To do this, the push_back() function can be used.

```
myVector.push_back(25);

//myVector now holds 25 in its first element

//push_back is called using the dot operator on the vector and we are passing in the value we want to
//be "pushed" on the vector
```

Now that the vector has 1 element we can index it with 0 as described above. We can also add as many elements to the vector as we like.

```
myVector.push_back(1);

myVector.push_back(5);

int x = 11;

myVector.push_back(x);

//myVector now holds 25,1,5,11 in that order
```

We can also retrieve the size of the vector using the size() function.

```
Int vectorSize=0;

vectorSize = myVector.size();

//vectorSize is now 4
```

(remember for indexing 4 elements, we use indexes of 0-3)

To get the first element of the vector we can use the begin() function instead of using an index of 0.

```
int first = myVector.begin();

//first is 25
```

So, what do we do if we want to erase an element?

Ex: erase first element

myVector.erase(myVector.begin());

//before this erase, vector holds 25,1,5,11

//after erase, vector holds 1,5,11

Ex: erase third element

myVector.erase(myVector.begin()+2);

//before erase vector holds 1,5,11

//after erase vector holds 1,5

//at an index of 0 the value is now 1 and at an index of 1 the value is 5

We cannot say:

myVector.erase(1);

You must use the .begin() function and use an offset.

Example 1:

```
vector<char> vec;
vec.push_back('h');
 vec.push_back('e');
vec.push_back('l');
vec.push_back('l');
vec.push_back('o');
vec[3] = 'p';
vec.erase(vec.begin()+4);
```

//at the end, the vector holds 'h', 'e', 'l', 'p'

Finally, another useful function for vectors is empty(). It returns true if the vector is empty or false if it is not.

If(!vec.empty()){

       //vector is not empty, do something

}

Static keyword

When the static keyword is used, the variable associated with it holds a special place in memory that is kept throughout the course of the program from the time it is created. So if you assign a value to a static variable, that value is retained till it is modified again. This is oppose to variables that have local scope which are created in certain parts of code and then the memory is released when the variable goes out of scope.

Example:

void staticTest();

 int main(){

       for(int i=0; i<3; i++){

              staticTest();

       }

       return 1;

}

void staticTest(){

       static int myStaticVar = 0;

       myStaticVar++;

       cout<<myStaticVar<<endl;

}

In this example, even though myStaticVar is locally declared, it holds a special place in memory where the value does not change unless explicitly changed over the entire execution of the application. So the outputted values of this sample are 1, 2, and 3. If the variable was not static, the function would always output 1 since the memory is allocated and deallocated every time the function is called and therefore the previous value assigned to that memory location is not retained.

#include and #define

In C++, the two primary files types for source code are header files (which have a .h extension) and source files (which have a .cpp extension). There is a #include statement that is placed in a header file or source file, usually at the beginning of the file and that tells the source if "include" a different header file. For example, if you wish to use the input/output filestreams in your source, then you would start that file with:

#include <iostream.h>

For header files that are already part of the library, the header file name is stated within <>. For, custom header files that you have coded, the header file is stated within " ". For example:

#include "myOwnHeaderFile.h"

Note, there is no semi-colon at the end of this statement. Also, what is happening is that the code in the header file is being "inserted" at that point in the source code that includes it. Furthermore, you could also #include a header file in another header file which is included in a .cpp file. Here is an example:

Header_1.h

//

int score = 0;

//

Header_2.h

//

#include "Header_1.h"

int lives = 5;

//

Main.cpp

//

```cpp
#include "Header_2.h"

int main(){
        score=200;
        lives-=1;
        return 1;
}
```

//

You can use #define in C++ to create a value that does not change by providing a name and the value. For example:

```cpp
#define PI 3.14

int main(){
        int radius = 2;
        double circleArea = PI * radius *radius;
        return 1;
}
```

You could also do this:

```cpp
#define WIDTH 10
#define LENGTH (WIDTH+5)
```

Notice, here also, there is no semi-colon which terminates the statement. The names of the used in #define also have global scope.

When dealing with many .cpp and .h files in your project, it may be a good idea to use #define. It can be used to avoid duplication of header files within the source code. If you have included the same header file more than once in another file, you may get errors such as a REDEFINITION error. An example on how to do this is:

Myheader.h

//

//place these statements at the beginning of this file

#ifndef MYHEADER_H   //if it is not already defined/used

#define MYHEADER_H   //then define it/use t

.

.

.

.

//at the end of the file, place this

#endif   //end of #ifndef

C-Strings

C-strings are simply character (char data type) arrays. So, for example, a C-string would be:

char avatarName[5];

avatarName[0] = 'F';

avatarName[1] = 'i';

avatarName[2] = 'z';

avatarName[3] = 'z';

avatarName[4] = '\0'; //null character, terminate the string cout<<avatarName; //outputs "Fizz"

as opposed to:

int x[3];

x[0] = 1;

x[1] = 2;

x[2] = 3;

cout<<x; //output is not 123

So, C-strings are simply ascii text made from character arrays. Remember that for a character array to put the null, \0, character at the end of it to terminate the string. Otherwise, you may get garbage data at the end of the string. C++ provides functions to work on character arrays. Another way C-strings are represented is within double quotes. So you can say:

cout<<"Hello World!";

In a character array, you need to terminate the string with a null character. When using double quotes, it is null terminated by default. However, when you store a double quoted string into a character array, you still need to terminate it with null at the appropriate element of the array.

Here are some different ways to store C-strings:

char weapon[4] = {'A','x','e','\0'};

char weapon2[10] = {'A','x','e','\0'};

both give the same output with cout. However, the array of size 10, you can still add new characters to it after the first 3 elements and overwrite the null character. Don't forget to place a null after the new characters you added.

char weapon3[10] = "Axe"; //this is also okay

You can also omit the array size if you initialize it as you are declaring it.

char weapon4[] = "Axe";

However, if you do this:

char weapon5[10] ;

weapon5 = "Axe"; //ERROR

you will get an error.

As mentioned earlier, there are string manipulation functions available via the cstring.h file.

1) strcpy(char * destination, const char * source)
   a. destination and source are strings
   b. what this does is copies the string frcm source to destination
   examples:

```
char myDest[10];
strcpy(myDest, "Hello");
```

or

```
char myDest[10];
char mySrc[6] = {'H','e','l','l','o','\0'};
strcpy(myDest, mySrc);
```

If you do this:

```
char myDest[5];
strcpy(myDest, "Hello");//ERROR because there is no room for the null character
```

2) strncpy(char * destination, const char * source, size_t length)

This is the same as strcpy, but specifies how many character to copy

Example:

```
char myDest[10];

strncpy(myDest, "testing", 4);

myDest[4] = '\0';//needed because null character not copied.

cout<<myDest;//outputs "test"
```

3) strcat(char * dest, const char * src)

This appends src to dest and the null character of dest is overwritten by the first character of src.

Example:

```
char s1[] = "Hello ";
char s2[] = "World";
strcat(s1, s2);
cout<<s2;//"World"
cout<<s1;//"Hello World"
```

4) strncat(char * dest, const char * src, size_t length)

This is the same as strcat but only append the number of characters specified from src to dest. Again, the null character is overwritten.

Example:

```
char s2[10] = {'D', 'o', '\0'};

strncat(s2, " it now", 3);

s[5]='\0';
```

5) strlen(const char * myString)

This function returns the length of the string before the null character.

Example:

```
int len = strlen("You shot the enemy");//len will be 18

char s3[10] = "shot";

int len2 = strlen(s3);//len2 will be 4
```

6) strcmp(const char *str1, const char *str2)

if str1 < str2, then returns a negative value

if str1 == str2, then returns 0

if str1 > str2, then returns a positive value

The protocol to determine this is:

    A) Check the first character of both strings

      a.   If the letter comes before the other in the ascii table then that string would be less (ie: "a" comes before "f", "A" comes before "a")

      b.   If the letters are the same, then check the next letter of both strings with the same rule

   B)   If one string is contained in the other, the longer one is greater

Examples:

int x = strcmp("alpha", "beta");//x is < 0

int x = strcmp("gamma", "gamma");//x is 0

int x = strcmp("chi-square", "chi");//x is > 0

7) strncmp(const char * s1, const char *s2, size_t length);

This will compare the string up to the number of characters specified.

Example:

int x = strcmp("chi-square", "chi", 3);// x is 0

Other useful functions that are part of stdlib.h:

1) int atoi(const char *str)

This will convert a string to an integer.

Examples:

int x = atoi("101");// x is 101

or...

char cnum[4] = "101";
int inum =atoi(cnum);//inum os 101 (integer)

2) char * itoa(int val, char *str, int base)

This will convert an integer into a string. However, it is only supported on some compilers.

Example:

int i=33;

char c[3];

itoa(i, c, 10);//c is "33" (string)

-binary is base 2

-octal is base 8

-decimal is base 10

-hexadecimal is base 16

3) sizeof(data)

This function will return the size in bytes of the passed parameter.

Examples:

int x=5;

int i = sizeof(x);//i is 4 (bytes)

char c[2] = {'H', '\0'};

int I = sizeof(c);//i is 2 (bytes), 1 byte per character

double y=3.14;

int i = sizeof(y);//i is 8 (bytes)

Pointers

A pointer is a memory address (points to a location in memory), and the address that is pointed to holds a value or some data. Like other variables, a pointer needs to be declared first. This is done with the asterisk operator.

EX:

int *myPointer;// could also be int* myPointer; or int * myPointer;

In this example, myPointer points to a memory location that holds data of type integer, which is noted by the int in the declaration.

You could also declare pointers to point to memory that holds different datatypes:

char *c;

double *d;

float *f;

Another operator that is used when reffering to memory address is the & operator. If you use & before a variable, it will yield the address of that variable.

So:

int x=5;

int *y;

0xAA12 [junk] y

The pointer, y, at address 0xAA12, does not point to anything meaningful yet...

0xBCCD [5] x

Here x holds the integer value 5 and is at memory location 0xBCCD.

If y is a memory address, and x is a place in memory that holds 5, then we can have y point to the address of x. The & operator is used to do this.

y = &x;//now y holds the address of x

so...

0xAA12 [0xBCCD] y

0xBCCD [5] x

Remember, y is not x. y is a pointer and x is not. x holds 5, and y holds the address of x. Furthermore, this applies to all data types.

EX:

char *c1;

char c2='!';

c1 = &c2;

0x0013 [0x1145] c1

0x1145 [!] c2

The question now is, what would need to be done if we wanted the use the pointer to see/retrieve the value of the location it points to. To do this, you need to use the dereferencing operator, *. So:

cout<<*c1;//would ouput "!"

cout<<c1;//would ouput 0x1145

With arrays we saw:

int myArr[10];

char myArr2[10];

myArr and myArr2 without indexing are pointers.

0x003F [0xABCD] myArr

0xABCD   [ ] myArr[0]

.   [ ] myArr[1]

.   [ ] myArr[2]

.   [ ] myArr[3]

.   [ ] myArr[4]

.   [ ] myArr[5]

.   [ ] myArr[6]

.   [ ] myArr[7]

.   [ ] myArr[8]

.   [ ] myArr[9]

Thus, myArr points to the first element in the array. myArr2 also points to it's first element in the array. So if we dereference with the * operator we get:

cout<<*myArr;//outputs the value in myArr[0]

However, if we output the pointers without dereferencing:

```
cout<<myArr;//outputs a memory address

cout<<myArr2;//will output a string
```

The character array outputs a string without dereferencing it is because character arrays are treated a little differently than other data types.

Pointers can also be used as return values of functions.

EX:

```
int *myfunc(int x);//function prototype

int main(){

        int *myPointer;

        int myVal = 4;

        myPointer = myfunc(myVal);

        cout<<*myPointer;//deferenced pointer, output is 4

        return 1;

}

int * myfunc(int valParm){

        int *temp;

        temp = &valParm;

        return temp;

}
```

///

```
char * myfunc2();


int main(){

        char *c;

        c = myfunc2();

        cout<<c;//outputs "Boss"
```

```cpp
        return 1;

}


char * myfunc2(){

        char c2[5] = {'B','o','s','s','\0'};

        return c2;

}
```

Pointers can also be used as function parameters.

EX:

```cpp
void myfunc3(int *x);

int main(){

        int y=277;

        int *z;

        z=&y;

        myfunc3(z);

        return 1;

}

void myfunc3(int *x){    //similar to call by reference as we are working with an address and not a copy

        int q=0;            //as in call by value

        q=*x+100;

        cout<<q;

}
//////////////////////////////////////////////////////////////////////////////////

void myfunc4(char *c);
```

```
int main(){

        char x[5] = {'B','o','s','s','\0'};

        myfunc4(x);

        return 1;

}
void myfunc4(char *c){

        cout<<c; //outputs "Boss"

}
```

If you simply declare a pointer without initializing it, it will initially hold "junk" data. It is sometimes a good idea to initialize the pointer to NULL.

int *p;

p = null;//now points to nothing rather than junk data

Till now, we saw pointers that were assigned a pointing address (memory location) of another variable:

int *p;

int q=24;

p=&q;

Dynamic variables are those created at runtime, not compile time, which means during execution of the program. Variables created at compile time are stored on the stack, and those at runtime are stored on the heap in memory.

COMPILE TIME   RUNTIME

STACK   HEAP

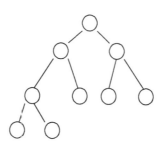

The way dynamic variables are created is with the new keyword.

EX:

int *p;

p = new int;   //new means dynamically allocate memory, and the int is the data type.

                    //It will work with its own memory space

*p=28;

0x33FA [0x33FF] p

0x33FF [28] (of type int)

This is different than before since now changing p does not change the variable it holds the address for when assigning it a value to it by dereferencing it since dynamically allocating memory for the pointer maintains its own address space. The following example shows how changing the pointer, changes the variable it holds the address for:

int *p;

p=null;

int x=5;

p=&x;

*p=28;//x changes to 28

There are good reasons for dynamically creating variables. For example, if you want to create an array that has a size that depends on the input during execution of the program, you would want to do this dynamically.

int input;

char *name;

cin>>input;

name = new char[input];//name becomes a character array with a size that is specified by input

When you use the new keyword to dynamically allocate memory, you need to use the delete keyword when you are done to free up that memory. Failing to use delete, can cause memory leaks and the heap can grow larger undesirably.

EX:

int *x;

x = new int;

delete x; //free the memory

char *c;

c = new char[5];

delete [] c; //placing the [] is required for arrays

int *x2;

x2 = new int[10];

delete [] x2;

File Input/Output

To perform input/output file operations the code needs to include <iostream> and <fstream.h>.

Hierarchy:

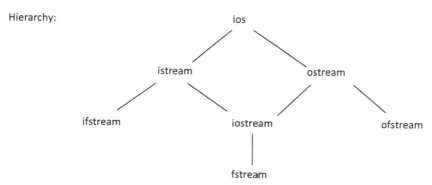

cin can also be used slightly differently than we have seen. It will depend on the input sentence to be terminated by END OF FILE, or, EOF.

char c = cin.get(); //gets one character at a time, loop this statement till c is equal to EOF

Another way to check if the input stream has reach the end of file is:

bool isEnd = cin.eof(); //returns true or false

cin also has a getline function. As oppose to cin.get(), which retrieves one character at a time, getline() will get the entire line until it sees a newline. Newline is a delimiter that is denoted by \n.

EX:

```
#include <iostream>

using namespace std;

int main(){

        int size=80;

        char buffer[size];

        cout<<"Enter a sentence: "<<endl;       //pressing ENTER after the input sentence places the
                                                //newline delimiter

        cin.getline(buffer, size);              //data stored in buffer as many character specified by
                                                //size, unless newline delimiter is seen first, in which
                                                //case it will store data/characters up to the delimiter

        cout<<buffer;

        return 1;

}
```

fstream.h allows file input and output. This can be reading data from a file (sequential access file). You will need to include the fstream header file:

#include <fstream.h>

The first thing that needs to be done is declaring the input file:

ifstream inputFile("myfile.txt");

Here, ifstream is the data type, inputFile is the name, and myfile.txt is the file that is being opened for reading.

After opening the file, check if it was successful:

if(!inputFile){

    //file could not be opened

}

If the file contains the data:

1	2	3
4	5	6
7	8	9

EOF

We can say:

int x[10];

int y[10];

int z[10];

int i=0;

while(inputFile>>x[i]>>y[i]>>z[i]){

    cout<<x[i]<<y[i]<<z[i]<<endl;

    i++;

}

This while loop will stop once it reaches the EOF. When you are done reading the file, call:

inputFile.close();

Furthermore, you can use .get() or .getline() with the input file stream. This is different than used before since now we are dealing with a file and not input from the console.

EX:

```
char buffer[10][50];

int i=0;

while(inputFile.getline(buffer[i], 50) != EOF){

        i++;

}
```

In this example, getline() will stop at the newline (\n) delimiter. However, you can also specify the delimiter for getline().

```
inputFile.getline(buffer, 10, ' ');
```

The 3rd parameter (space) is the specified delimiter instead of \n. Therefore it will stop when it sees a space in the input. When it stops at this delimiter it will extract it, then discard it. Next time it is called, it will start where it left off (after the delimiter). Similarly, .get() can be used with fstream.

EX:

```
ifstream inputF("myfile2.txt");

char c[100]; //create character array of 100 elements. Do not know how many characters are in file

int i = 0;

while(!inputF.eof()){

        c[i] = inputF.get();

}

inputF.close();
```

Some other useful file stream functions:

.peek()

     -"peeks" at the next character in the stream but does not extract it.

.tellg()

     -returns length of the file at current position in the file

.seekg(offset, direction)

-direction to seek. Can be ios:beg, for the beginning of the file, ios::end for the end of the file, or ios:cur for the current position in the file.

-offset is how much to offset relative to the direction.

EX:

```
inputF.seekg(0, ios::end);// place "cursor" at end of the file

int length = inputF.tellg();//get the length of the file

inputF.seekg(0, ios:beg);//go back to the beginning of the file

char buffer = new char[length];
```

.putback(char)

-puts back the character passed as a parameter into the stream's current location

-will be read at next input stream operation

So far, we have looked at input file streams. There are also output file streams using ofstream.

```
ofstream outputFile("out.txt");

if(!outputFile){

        //could not open file

}

outputFile<<'a'<<'\n';

outputFile<<'b'<<'\n';

outputFlle<<'c'<<'\n';


outputFile.close();
```

The output file can be opened in different ways. The way shown above is the default and uses ios:out, which means to write to the file from the beginning of the file. It is synonymous to:

```
ofstream outputF("out.txt", ios:out);
```

Alternatively, instead of ios::out, ios::app can be used to open the file and start writing to it from the end of the file, thus, appending to it.

EX: (copy contents of one file to another file)

```
ifstream inFile("in.txt");

ofstream outFile("out.txt");

if(inFile && outFile){

        char buffer;

        while(!inFile.eof()){

                buffer = inFile.get();

                outFile<<buffer;

        }

inFile.close();

outFile.close();
```

Function Pointers

A function pointer is simply a pointer, as we have seen, that points to a function. Function definitions are also stored in memory and the function pointer holds the address of the memory location of the function. Event driven functions and callback functions are based on function pointers.

Function pointers also need to be declared like regular functions. The function pointer is used to point to any other function as long as the signatures are the same. Thus, it can perform different operations depending on the function it is pointing to. This occurs at runtime and therefore the same function pointer can point to different functions, which have their own definitions, during the course of the program. When it points to a particular function, and it is called, it is as if the function that is pointed to is executed. The function pointer does not have its own definition.

EX:

```
int add(int, int);

int subtract(int, int);

int (*doMath)(int, int);//function pointer declaration, same signature as add or subtract
```

```cpp
int main(){
        int operation=0;
        int num1=0;
        int num2=0;
        int result=0;
        cout<<"Enter 1 to add or 2 to subtract:"<<endl;
        cin>>operation;
        cout<<"enter first operand:"<<endl;
        cin>>num1;
        cout<<"enter second operand:"<<endl;
        cin>>num2;
        if(operation==1){
                doMath = &add; //assign the address of add to the function pointer
        }
        else if(operation==2){
                doMath = &subtract;//assign address of subtract to function pointer
        }
        result = doMath(num1, num2);
        cout<<"The result is: "<<result;
        return 1;
}
int add(int x, int y){
        return x+y;
}
int subtract(int x, int y){
```

```
        return x-y;

}
```

Bitwise Operations

In Chapter 1 boolean logic was discussed. These Boolean operations, such as AND, OR, XOR, can also be applied in code. These are also known an bitwise operations, operations on bits which hold a value of 0 or 1. Here are the operators to use in code to perfrorm the bitwise operations:

    &   AND

    | OR

    ^   XOR

    <<   left shit the first operand by the number of places of the second operand and fill zeros

        EX:

        unsigned short x = 1;

        x<<1

        Initial – 00000000 00000001

        After – 00000000 00000010

    >>   right shift

    ~   one's compliment (all zeros become ones and all ones become zero)

        EX:

        unsigned short x = 5; // 00000000 00000101

        ~x; //11111111 11111010

EX:

#include<iostream>

```cpp
#include <iomanip>

using namespace std;

void displaybits(unsigned short);

int main(){

        unsigned short x;

        cout<<"Enter number:"<<endl;

        cin>>x;

        displaybits(x);

        return 0;

}

void displaybits(unsigned short value){

        unsigned short c;

        unsigned short displaymask = 1<<15;

        for(c=1; c<16; c++){

                if(value & displaymask){

                        cout<<'1';

                }

                else{

                        cout<<'0';

                }

                value<<=1;

        }

}
//value & displaymask will be 10000000 0000000, which is TRUE, or 00000000 00000000, which is FALSE
//by doing this, this example will output the binary version of the parameter for displaybits.
```

Chapter 4: Object Oriented Programming in C++

Object oriented programming is primarily about creating custom data types. The three most important properties of object oriented programming are abstraction, encapsulation, and inheritance. Abstraction is creating a customer data type where the information about it is hidden. Thus, the details are not revealed. Encapsulation is the idea where multiple properties of the custom data type are grouped in a certain way. Finally, inheritance is a technique where data is shared and derivation can occur. I will go into more detail about inheritance later.

Structs

The custom data type is called a class in object oriented programming in C++. Classes do not exist in C, but C and C++ share another type of custom data type called a struct. The definition of a struct is a data type that contains related items of different data types. If you had an array of doubles, then every element of the array is of a double data type. Here is an example of a struct:

struct Warrior{ //struct keyword required, the struct name is Warrior

bool hasWeapon;

int health;

double money;

}; //end the curly brace with a semi-colon

So you can see that different data of different data types are combined into a single entity called "Warrior". You can have as many items of any data types grouped into a struct. After you have defined the struct, you need to declare a variable of the type just like any other variable.

Warrior Conan; //the variable is Conan that is of data type Warrior

Through the variable, you can access the variables that are part of the struct definition. This means you can get or set, hasWeapon, health, and money, through the variable, Conan. This is done using the dot (.) operator.

```
Conan.hasWeapon = false;

Conan.health = 100;

Conan.money =200.5;

//some code

if(Conan.health<=0){

        //game over

}
```

You can also have structs within structs. For example:

```
struct Avatar{

        Warrior myWarrior;

        bool firstPersonMode;

};

Avatar Fizz;

Fizz.myWarrior.hasWeapon = true;

Fizz.myWarrior.health = 100;

Fizz.myWarrior.money=0.0;

Fizz.firstPersonMode = false;

//some code

if(LeftMousePress==true){

        Fizz.firstPersonMode = true;

}

if(Fizz.firstPersonMode==true){

        //change camera
```

```
}

if(EnemyAttack()==true){

        Fizz.myWarrior.health-=10;

}
```

Classes

A class is very similar to a struct. Like "struct", "class" is also a keyword.

```
class myClass{

        //member functions and member variables

};
```

Classes are used for real-world modeling.   It defines something that has properties and actions/behavior. For example, an apple can be made into a class. It's properties would be that it is round and red. The actions/behavior would be that it crunches when bitten, it grows on trees, and gets spoiled when not eaten.   Thus, the properties of a class are member variables, and the behavior is defined by member functions.   As mentioned in the beginning of the chapter, the three main phenomena of classes encapsulation, inheritance, and polymorphism.

For encapsulation, a class combines attributes and behavior into one entity, a class. An instance of a class is called an object. Just like if we created a variable of data type integer, an object is like a variable of a custom data type, that which is defined by the class definition. This custom data type has both related variables and related functions. So, given the example code above, we can say:

```
myClass myObject;
```

myObject is an instance of myClass and can be named any valid variable name. Classes also allow information hiding, which is also part of encapsulation. This means that parts of the code in the class, are hidden from the rest of the program.   Since classes have attributes and behavior, we can declare variables and functions in the class. These are known as member variables and member functions. For example:

```
class myClass{

        int x; //cannot initialize here

        int y; // cannot initialize here

        void increment_x(); //function prototype
```

```
void add_to_y(int); //function prototype
```

```
};
```

By default, all the members of a class are private. This means that they cannot be accessed by code that is outside of the class. To make the members accessible from code outside of the class definition, you use the keyword "public". For example:

```
class myClass{

public:

        int x;

        int y;

        void increment_x();

        void add_to_y(int);

};
```

Now these members can be accessed outside of the class, but by using the object, an instance of the class.

EX:

```
int main(){

        myClass myObject;

        myObject.x = 0;

        myObject.y = 1;

        myObject.increment_x();

        myObject.add_to_y(5);


        return 1;

}
```

Public vs. Private Members

Note, that the dot operator is used for accessing members like it was for structs. Also, we have called the member functions, but they are not defined yet. Furthermore, the dot operator can be used to access the members since they are all "public". If they were left as default without specifying the scope (private) then this would not be possible and you would get compile time errors. If they were private, then access is allowed only inside the class. The following example is legal:

```
class test{

        int x;

        int add_to_x(int z){

                x+=z;

                return x;

        }

};
```

Here, the member function is defined inside the class and the private member variable can be accessed by the member function inside the class.

Members can be combined as "public" and "private". If this is done, you must specify which members are public and which ones are private.

EX:

```
class myNumberOperations{

public:

        void increment_x();

        int add_to_y(int);

private:

        int x;

        int y;

};
```

```
int main(){

        int num;

        myNumberOperations myNumOps;

        myNumOps.increment_x(); //legal

        num = myNumOps.add_to_y(5); //legal

        myNumOps.x=0; //illegal

        myNumOps.y=4; //illegal

        return 1;

}
```

In the class above, there are function prototypes, but no definition. Usually, classes are broken into a header file (.h), for the class definition, and a source (.cpp) file for the function definitions for the member functions of the class. However, this does not mean that the member function definition cannot be inside the class itself. The general rule is that if the function definition is short, include it in the class, but if it is long define it in a corresponding source file.

EX:

```
//////myClass2.h//////////////header file

class myClass2{

public:

        void increment_x();

        int add_to_y(int);

private:

        int x;

        int y;

};

//////////////myClass2.cpp//////////source file

#include "myClass2.h"

void myClass2::increment_x(){
```

```
        x++;

}

int myClass2::add_to_y(int i){

        y+=i;

        return y;

}
```

////////////////////////////////////

In this example, for the first function defined, void is the function return type, myClass2 is the class name, :: is the access operator, and increment_x() is the function name. The variable, x, that is being incremented by this function is the same member variable of the class. It will retain it's value for the lifetime of the object.

/////////////////////main.cpp////////////////////////////////

```
#include <iostream>

#include "myClass2.h"

using namespace std;

int main(){

        myClass2 class2;

        int z;

        class2.increment_x();

        z = class2.add_to_y(7);

        cout<<z;

        return 1;

}
```

///

If this is done, what would the value of z be after the member function add_to_y, returns? The answer is that you will see "junk" data. This is because y, and for that matter, x, were never initialized to a value. When they are only declared, they hold "junk" data and therefore, no matter what you add to it, will also be "junk" data. However, when and where in the class the variables are declared, they cannot, by rule, be initialized. So the question is how are we supposed to initialize the member variables. The answer is by using a function called a constructor.

The Constructor

A constructor always has the same name as the class. There are two types of contructors. The first is called the default constructor and then there are all other contructors (those that take parameters). The default constructor also does not take any parameters.

EX:

class myClass3{

public:

        myClass3(); //default constructor, same name as class, no parameters

        myClass3(int param1, int param2);

        void increment_x();

        int add_to_y(int i);

private:

        int x;

        int y;

};

/////////////////////constructor definitions in corresponding cpp file/////////////////

myClass3::myClass3(){ //default constructor definition, no return value

        x=0; //initialize x to 0

        y=1; //initialize y

}

myClass3::myClass3(int param1, int param2){

        x=param1; //initialize to value of first parameter

        y = param2; //initialize to value of second parameter

}

// other member function defined like before by using myClass3

//

Now, when the object/s are created it/they can use the default constructor or the non-default constructor. For example:

myClass3 class3; /*instance of myClass3 that will use the default constructor, x and y initialized(no parenthesis)*/

myClass3 class3b(7,9); //object created where x is initialized to 7 and y to 9

//myClass4.h///

```cpp
class myClass4{

public:

        myClass4();

        myClass4(int, int);

        void incrementX();

        int getX();

        int addToY(int);

private:

        int x;

        int y;

};
```

//function definitions in myClass4.cpp

///

//////////////////main.cpp//

#include "myClass4.h"

```cpp
#include <iostream>

using namespace std;


int main(){

        myClass4 moneyPouch1;

        myClass4 moneyPouch2(7,9);

        int diamonds1, diamonds2, rubies1, rubies2;


        moneyPouch1.incrementX();

        diamonds1 = moneyPouch1.getX();

        rubies1 = moneyPouch1.addToY(10);


        moneyPouch2.incrementX();

        diamonds2 = moneyPouch2.getX();

        rubies2 = moneyPouch2.addToY(10);


        cout<<"In first pouch there are "<<diamonds1<<" diamonds, and "<<rubies1<<" rubies."<<endl;

        cout<<"In 2nd pouch there are "<<diamonds2<<" diamonds, and "<<rubies2<<" rubies."<<endl;

        return 1;

}
```

When creating objects of the same class, you can copy the values from one object to the other. This is done via the assignment operator. For example:

```cpp
myClass4 a;

myClass4 b;

a = b;
```

After doing this, a will have the values that b has at the time of assignment.

Static : revisited

We saw earlier what the static keyword was and how it works. Static member functions and member variables work the same way. Static members exist even if an object does not exist. To call the static member, use the following notation:

classname:mystaticmembervar;//static member variable

classname:mystaticmemberfunc();//static member function

Also, all objects of the same class use the same memory location for the static members.

For example:

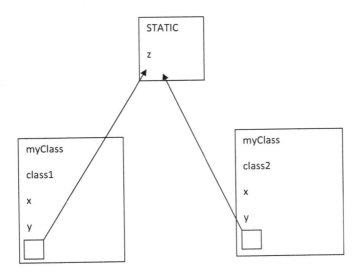

If a member variable is declared as static, it must be defined before usage outside the class. Furthermore, static member functions can only access static member variables.

```
//program.cpp

class staticTest{

        static int myStaticMember;

        static int reset(){ return 0;}

};

int staticTest::myStaticMember=1;

void main(){

        staticTest::myStaticMember=staticTest::reset();

        int temp = staticTest::myStaticMember; //temp stores '0' now

}
```

Instantiation

Creating an object is called Instantiation. This can be done via the default constructor or any other constructor in a class.

```
myClass myClass1; //default constructor

myClass myClass2(5,4);//other constructor
```

Instantiating an object this way occurs at compile time and is stored on the stack in memory. Creating and object (instantiation) can also be done dynamically, or at run-time. At run-time the object is stored on the heap in memory. Dynamic instantiation, or dynamic memory allocation is done via the *new* keyword.

EX:

myClass *dynObj; //(pointer)

//dynamically allocate memory for the pointer to an object via the new keyword and the constructor

dynObj = new myClass();

This can also be done on a single line of code:

myClass *dynObj = new myClass();

One reason for storing the object on the heap at run-time as opposed to on the stack at compile-time is because this way run-time input can determine memory allocation and execution. In other words, this is important if input to the application is used to "define" the objects and reduce the stack size. For example, the user input can be the parameter values into the constructor. This can only be done if the object is created dynamically.

Introduction to Inheritance

Inheritance is an object oriented characteristic that allows classes to be derived from other classes. For example, there may be a child class that is derived from a parent class. The child class "inherits" members of the parent class. There are three types of inheritance; public, protected, and private.

EX: Public Inheritance

//classParent.h

class classParent{

public:

```cpp
        void func1(){
                x=y+z;
        }
        int func2();
protected:
        int x;
        int y:
        bool z;
private:
        double q;
};
//classChild.h
#include "classParent.h" //necessary
class classChild : public classParent{
public:
        void func3(){
                r=x+y+z;//OK, x,y,z are inherited as protected members
        }
private:
        int r;
};
```

In public inheritance, public member of the parent become public members of the child. This means that they are accessible from within the class and outside the class. Protected members of the parent become protected members of the child. Private members of the parent are not inherited.

Protected member functions or member variables are similar to private members in that they can only be accessed from within the class (member functions but not through the object) with the difference only in how those member are inherited. This difference is that regardless of the type of inheritance(public, protected, private), private members are never inherited. Protected members are inherited by the child class as protected members in public inheritance, as protected in protected inheritance, and as private members in private inheritance.

A child class can have its own public, protected, and private members. From the sample code above:

classParent *class_p = new classParent();

classChild *class_c = new classChild();

class_p->func1(); //OK

class_p->func2();//OK

class_p->x; //ERROR, protected

class_p->q; //ERROR, private

class_c->func3();//OK

class_c->func1();//OK, inherited

class_c->func2();//OK, inherited

class_c->x; //ERROR, inherited but protected

class_c->q;   //ERROR, not inherited in child class and private (cannot access through object in parent
                 //class)

Modular Design

Class definitions are usually done in header files (.h extension). Member function definitions are usually done in source files (.cpp extension). Other than the extension, the header file name and the source file name should match. Also, if you have an instance of one class in another class, you need to include the header file for that class. For example:

```
//class1.h/////////////////////////
class class1{
//member functions and variables
};
```

```
//class1.cpp/////////////////////////
void class1::myfunc(){
//some code
}
```

```
//class2.h/////////////////////////
#include "class1.h"
class class2{
public:
        //members
private:
        class1 *myClass1;
        //other members
};
```

```
//main.cpp//////////////////////////
#include "class1.h"
#include "class2.h"
int main(){
//code
}
```

When working with multiple header files that need to be included, repetition needs to be avoided (including the header file more than once). In the above example, in main.cpp class1 and class2 header files have been included, but class2's header file already includes class1.h and therefore class1.h has been included more than once in main.cpp. This can cause re-definition problems with the compiler. To avoid this we can start and end the header file with the following example code:

```
//class1.h/////////////////////
#ifndef CLASS1_H
#define CLASS1_H
class class1{
//code
};
#endif
```

Here we are saying that if this class have not been defined, then use the following code, but if it has been defined, then do not. Thus, if this is done, in main.cpp the class1.h file is only "seen" once even if it has been included.

Dynamic Memory Allocation

Dynamically allocating memory occurs at runtime and is stored on the heap as oppose to occurring at compile time on the stack. There are many instances of where we would prefer to dynamically allocate memory rather than statically. An example is that there is an application where the user needs to enter a number from 1 to 3. Depending on what was entered, we will need to use the appropriate object. If this is done statically, it would be necessary to create all three objects up front. Thus, there are 3 different constructors required.

```
myClass1 class1;

myClass1 class1b(5,4);

myClass1 class1c(3.0, 4,1);
```

So how do we know which object to use once they are ALL created based on the input which occurs at runtime? We could...

```
if(x==1){

        class1.someFunc();

}
else if(x==2){

        class1b.someFunc();

}
else{

        class1c.someFunc();

}
```

This type of check will be necessary throughout the code every time you wish to access the appropriate object. The problems with this approach are:

1) Three unnecessary objects are created (only one is needed for each time the application is run). This is a waste of memory.
2) There is extra coding involved

3) There is extra processing and thus cause the application to run slower

The way to solve this problem is to use dynamic memory allocation using pointers! Using pointers, we can…

```
myClass1 *class1;

if(x==1){

        class1 = new myClass1();

}

else if(x==2){

        class1 = new myClass1(5,4);

}

else{

        class1 = new myClass1(3.0, 4,1);

}
```

The code above (conditional check to create object) only needs to be done once, as oppose to every time the correct object needs to be used (as in static allocation). This means faster execution time. When the object needs to be accessed, we can simply use class1 which is already created according to the user input (no conditional check needed). Furthermore, it is more memory efficient as only one object is created rather than three.

The notation for accessing public members of a pointer to an object is:

```
(*class1).someFunc();
```

Or

```
class1->someFunc(); //arrow notation
```


These 2 different notation do the same thing and are both valid.

EX:

```
class car{
public:

        car(); //constructor

        ~car(); //destructor

        int getSpeed(){return speed;}

        void setSpeed(int x){speed=x;}
private:

        int speed;
};
```

Question: How do we instantiate dynamically?

```
        car *porshe = new car();
```

Question: How do we set speed?

```
        porshe->setSpeed(200);
```

Question: How do we get speed?

```
        int y=0;

        y=porshe->getSpeed();
```

Question: can we access private members?

```
        porshe->speed=300; //ERROR, still cannot access private members!
```

Question: if speed was protected instead of private, could we access it via the pointer?

        NO! Same as private scope but differs when using inheritance.

We have seen that a class can have public, protected, and private members. It can have all, only two, or just one. If public, protected, or private is not specified for the members, then by default they are considered private.

The Destructor

When you dynamically allocate memory with the new keyword, you need to free that memory when the object is no longer needed or the application ends. Failing to do so will cause memory leaks. Freeing dynamically allocated memory is done by the delete keyword.

EX:

car *porshe = new car();

//some code

delete porshe; //object no longer needed, free the memory

The delete keyword implicitly calls the destructor. The destructor can be defined also to perform any other cleanup operations. The destructor syntax is that of the default constructor with a tilde (~) preceding it.

~car();

Another example is:

class test{

public:

        test();//constructor

        ~test();//destructor

        double getResult();

private:

        double result;

};

The destructor is not only called when 'deleting' the object, but also when the object goes out of scope.

Overloaded Functions

An overloaded function is a member function that has the same name as another member function, but has a different signature. The signature of a function consists of the function name and the parameter list.

If we had the following 2 member functions:

class test{

public:

      void myFunc1();

      void myFunc2();

};

The compiler has no problem with this since the function name is different. But what if we wanted to use the same name for functions? Then, we would need to 'overload' the function by changing the parameter list.

class test2{

public:

      void myFunc(int x); //(a)

      void myFunc(int x, int y); //(b)

};

The compiler also has no issue with this even though the names are the same since the parameter list is different and thus the signature is different (name + parameter list). This is called function overloading. When we call the function (like this):

test2 testing;

testing.myFunc(3,2);

The compiler sees that we are passing two parameters and thus know to use function (b). However, doing the following will return a compiler error because the compiler will look at the function name and parameter only, not the return type.

class test3{

public:

```
    void myfunc(int x);

    int myfunc(int x);

};
```

Having more than one constructor is a type of overloaded function. Recall, you can have multiple constructors; one as the default constructor with no parameters, and others with different parameters.

```
class test4{

public:

    test4(); //default constructor

    test4(int x);

    test4(int x, int y);

};
```

Not only can you have overloaded functions, overloading operators is also possible. This means changing the meaning and usage of the operator being overloaded. Some examples of operators that can be overloaded are: +, -, /, *, <<, >>, <, >, ==, >=

Only existing operators can be overloaded. New operators cannot be created. To overload an operator, a function is required. The syntax of the function to overload an operator is:

returnType operator operatorSymbol(formal parameter list)

-returnType is what the function returns

-operator is a keyword

-operatorSymbol is the symbol of the operator to be overloaded

-formal parameter list is the parameters that the function uses

In object oriented programming, the keyword 'this' refers to the object itself. 'this' is a pointer to the object and refers the the object in it's entirety. The 'this' pointer can be useful in various cases and also useful when overloading operators. A simple example that uses the 'this' point is:

```cpp
//my.h file
class test{
public:
        test update(int x, int y);
private:
        int q;
        int r;
};
//my.cpp file
test test::update(int x, int y){
        q=x;
        r=y;
        return *this;
}
//main.cpp file
#include "my.h"
void main(){
        test test1;
        test test2;
        test1 = test2.update(5,4);
}
```

Member overloaded operator example:

```
//op.h
class rectangle{
public:
        rectangle(){}
        rectangle(double l, double w){
                length=l; width=w;
        }
        rectangle operator+(const rectangle&);
        rectangle operator*(const rectangle&);
        bool operator==(const rectangle&);
private:
        double length;
        double width;
};
//op.cpp
rectangle rectangle::operator+(const rectangle& rectangle2){
        rectangle newrect;
        newrect.length = length + rectangle2.length;
        newrect.width = width + rectangle2.width;
        return newrect;
}
rectangle rectangle::operator*(const rectangle& rectangle2){
        rectangle newrect;
        newrect.length = length * rectangle2.length;
```

```cpp
        newrect.width = width * rectangle2.width;

        return newrect;

}

bool rectangle::operator==(const rectangle& rectangle2){

        if((length==rectangle2.length)&&(width==rectangle2.width)){

                return true;

        }

        else{

                return false;

        }

}

//main.cpp

#include "op.h"

#include <iostream>

using namespace std;

void main(){

        rectangle rect1(5,6);

        rectangle rect2(3,7);

        rectangle rect3;

        rectangle rect4;

        rect3 = rect1 + rect2;    //overloaded operator used.   Return type of the overloaded '+'
                                  //operator is a rectangle.  If '+' was not overloaded, this would be a
                                  //compiler error.  rect3's length and width are the addition of rect1 and
                                  //rect2's length and width like specified in the definition. The compiler
                                  //sees the left-hand-side and the right-hand-side of the '+' operator as
                                  //type rectangle and knows to use the overloaded operator.

        rect4 = rect1 * rect2; //uses '*' overloaded operator
```

```cpp
if(rect3==rect4){ //uses '==' overloaded operator

        cout<<"Rectangles are equal"<<endl;

}

else{

        cout<<"Rectangles are not equal"<<endl;

}

}
```

If an overloaded operator function is not a member function, then the parameter list would need to change if it is to be used for a left-hand-side object and a right-hand-side object. As seen above, since the overloaded operator function was a member of a class, the left-hand-side was accounted for.

X = LHS + RHS;

Thus, the syntax of the prototytpe would be:

friend returnType operator#(const className& firstObject, const className& secondObject);

//'friend' is a keyword

A usage example would be:

newObject = firstObject # secondObject;

For member overloaded operators, the 'this' pointer can also be used. For example:

```cpp
class rectangle{

public:

        rectangle(int l, int w){length = l; width=w}

        void operator+(const rectangle& rectangle2){

                this->length = length + rectangle2.length;

                this->width = width + rectangle2.width;

        }
```

```
private:

        int length;

        int width;

};


void main(){

        rectangle rect1(5,4);

        rectangle rect2(3,7);

        rect1 + rect2;    //do not need to assign to another object.  rect1 now holds the final values
                          //because that is how the function is defined with no return type.

}
```

Inheritance Revisited

Earlier in the chapter we saw 'public' inheritance. There are two other types of inheritance. There is also 'protected' and 'private' inheritance. In all types of inheritance, when creating or instantiating objects, the Parent class constructor is called first, and then the child or derived class constructor is called.

Public Inheritance:

Parent class members:	public	protected	private
Child class inherits as:	public	protected	Not inherited

Protected Inheritance:

Parent class members:	public	protected	private
Child class inherits as:	protected	protected	Not inherited

Private Inheritance:

Parent class members:	public	protected	private
Child class inherits as:	private	private	Not inherited

Protected inheritance syntax:

```
class B: protected A{
        ...
```

Private inheritance syntax:

```
class B: private A{
        ...
```

A child class may also become the parent class for another child class. For example:

```
class A{
public:
        A();
        void func();
protected:
        int x;
private:
        int y;
};
class B: public A{
public:
        B();
        void func2();
protected:
        double z;
private:
        bool q;
```

```cpp
};

class C: public B{
public:
        C();
        void func3();
protected:
        int r;
private:
        bool s;
};
/////////////////////////////////////////////////
C obj3;
obj3.func(); //ok
obj3.func2(); //ok
obj3.func3(); //ok
obj3.r=5; //error
/////////////////////////////////////////////////////
void C::func3(){
        r=x; //ok
        r=y; //error
        r=z; //ok
        s=q; //error
        s=true; //ok
}
```

The same concept applies no matter how many child classes there are.

B inherits from A, C inherits from B, and therefore C inherits from A. This is 'is a' relationship.

It is also possible for multiple inheritance. This is where a child class inherits from multiple parent classes. For example:

```
class Parent1{

public:

        Parent1();

        ~Parent1();

        void func1();

protected:

        int x;

};
//////////////////////////////////////////////////
class Parent2{

public:

        Parent2();

        ~Parent2();

        void func2();

protected:

        int y;

};
//////////////////////////////////////////////////
class child1: public Parent1, public Parent2{

public:
```

```cpp
        child1();

        ~child();

        void func3();
private:

        int z;
};
////////////////////////////////////////////////////////////
int main(){

        Parent1 p1;

        Parent2 p2;

        child1 c1;

        p1.func1(); //ok

        p1.func2(); //error

        p1.func3(); //error

        p2.func1(); //error

        p2.func2(); //ok

        c1.func1(); //ok

        c1.func2(); //ok

        c1.func3(); //ok

        return 1;
}

////////////////////////////////////////////////////////////
void child1::func3(){

        z=x+y; //ok since x is inherited from Parent1, y from Parent2, and z is child1's private member
}
```

The order in which the constructors are called is first from the parent class and then the child class. The destructor order is first from the child class and then the parent class.

Overriding Functions

A child class can have the same function (with the same signature) as its parent class. However, the function definition in the child class is different. This is called function overriding.

Example:

```
class A{

public:

        int myfunc(){

                return x;

        }

private:

        int x;

};


class B:public A{

public:

        int myfunc(){

                return y;

        }

private:
```

```
        int y;

};


int main(){

        A a;

        B b;

        int q,r;

        q=a.myfunc();

        r=b.myfunc();

        //the compiler knows which function to call based on the object that called it.

        return 1;

}
```

'has a' Relationship

A 'has a" relationship is where there is an instance of a class in another class. Let us say that myclass1 is already defined. Then, we can include myclass1 in another class as a member.

```
///////myclass2.h/////////////////////////////////////////

#include "myclass1.h"

class myclass2{

public:

        myclass2();

        myclass1 func1();
```

```cpp
        void func2(myclass c);

private:

        myclass1 a;

};
///////////myclass2.cpp/////////////////////////////////
#include "myclass2.h"

myclass1 myclass2::func1(){

        return a;

}
/////////////main.cpp/////////////////////////////////
 #include "myclass2.h"

int main(){

        myclass1 c1;

        myclass2 c2;

        c1 = c2.func1();

        c2.func2(c1);

        return 1;

}
```

Polymorphism and Virtual Functions

Polymorphism is where an object can take many forms. This is usually accomplished via a pointer to the object and is based on inheritance principles. Thus, a parent class pointer can point to a child class object.

Ex:

class Enemy{

```
...

};


class Boss: public Enemy{

...

};


Enemy *pBoss = new Boss(); //Enemy pointer points to a Boss object
```

Polymorphism is very useful and powerful. When designing a game with enemies, the enemies can be of type 'Boss', 'Special Boss', and 'zombies', for example. These types of enemies can all inherit from the 'Enemy' parent class and therefore inherit member variables and functions from the parent class that all the child classes do not have to re-implement (although each one can redefine them).

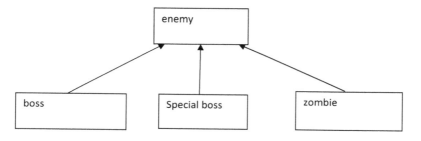

If we had a function that checked collisions with all enemies, we have to keep track of each type and number of that type of enemy if we did not use polymorphism.

```
Boss b1;

Boss b2;

Special_Boss sb;

zombie z1;

zombie z2;
```

//will need to know this information when calling the collision function

It would be easier to just check the generic enemy list since it is the parent class of all the child classes. With polymorphism this would prove to be much easier.

Enemy *myList[5];

myList[0] = new Boss();

myList[1] = new Boss();

myList[2] = new Special_Boss();

myList[3] = new zombie();

myList[4] = new zombie();

Now, when we can call the collision function, we can simply check the myList array instead of each individual object where we would also need to know the type. If we need a function that needs to take in a parameter of type Boss, Special_Boss, or zombie, polymorphism comes in handy again.

bool checkCollision(Enemy *e);

With something like this, we can pass in all the types that inherit from Enemy. The pointer type is still Enemy, but the object type is Boss, Special_Boss, and zombie. If we did not use polymorphism, we would need three different functions.

bool checkCollision(Boss *b);

bool checkCollision(Special_Boss *sb);

bool checkCollision(zombie *z);

It does not work the other way around.

Boss *b = new Enemy(); //error

Virtual functions are tied to inheritance and polymorphism. This is where the parent class and child class have the same function with the same signature.

class A{

public:

        void print();

};

```
class B:public A{
public:
        void print();
};
```
///
```
void A::print(){
        cout<<"Hello";
}
```
///
```
void B:print(){
        cout<<"World";
}
```
///
```
A a;
B b;
a.print(); //prints "Hello"
b.print(); //prints "World"
```


If we used polymorphism:

A *test = new B();

And then did:

test->print();

It would still call the parent class's print function and the output would be "Hello".

RULE: if a function in the parent/base class is not labeled as 'virtual' the function of the class of the pointer type is always called. (in this example 'A' is the pointer type)

If we want to call the function of the object type class, we need to declare the function as 'virtual' in the parent class.

```
class A{

public:

        virtual void print();

};
```

```
class B:public A{

public:

        void print();

};
```

```
A *test = new B();
```

test->print(); //now print is called from class B and the output is "World"

However, if we needed to call the print function from the parent class, we would explicitly need to call it.

test->A::print() ;//outputs "Hello"

The print function in the child class B, can be labeled with or without the virtual keyword and the result would be the same. The only purpose of including the virtual keyword in the child class is so someone looking at the code will know that it is a virtual function.

Destructors Revisited

A rule of thumb is that if a class had a pointer as a member variable, then the class needs a destructor. The destructor is called when the object goes out of scope or when the delete keyword is used on the object.

Example:

```
class dTest{
public:
        dTest(){
                a = new A();
                b = new B();
        }
        ~dTest(){
                delete a;
                delete b;
        }
private:
        A *a;
        B *b;
};

///////////////////////////////////////////////

dTest *dt = new dTest();

...

delete dt; //explicit call to the destructor
```

However, there is a problem. If a function has a formal parameter of a base class, and we pass in a derived class object (we can do this because of polymorphism), then when the object goes out of scope, the base class destructor is called. What about destroying the derived class object? The solution is to have a virtual destructor. To do this, the destructor in the base class needs to be declared as virtual (like we saw with functions). When we do this, the destructor in the derived class gets called when the object goes out of scope, and then the base class destructor is called. If the destructor was not virtual, only the base class destructor would be called.

Ex:

```cpp
class Car{
public:
        Car();
        virtual ~Car();
        virtual void print();
};


class Mustang:public Car{
public:
        Mustang();
        ~Mustang();
        virtual void print();
};
//////////////////////////////////////////
void getSpeed(Car *c);
void main(){
        Car *myCar = new Mustang();
        void getSpeed(myCar);
}




void getSpeed(Car *c){
        c->print();
}//after the function returns the Mustang destructor gets called first and then the Car destructor
//because it was declared 'virtual'.
```

Abstract Base Class & Pure Virtual Functions

Sometimes we want to create a base class that is used in inheritance but you do not want to be able to create an object of that class (only there so derived classes can inherit members). It also should not define functionality. For this, an abstract base class is used. An abstract base class must contain one or more pure virtual functions. A pure virtual function is a virtual function in an abstract base class that has no definition.

Ex:

class Ball{ //abstract base class, cannot create object of type Ball

public:

        virtual void motion()=0; //pure virtual function, no definition

        virtual void calcForce()=0; //pure virtual function

protected:

        int mass;

};

class football: public Ball{

public:

        void motion(){

                //motion defined here

        }

        void calcForce(){

                //calcForce defined here

        }

};

class baseball:public Ball{

public:

```
    void motion(){
            //motion defined here
    }
    void calcForce(){
            //calcForce defined here
    }
};
```

There are no function definitions in the Ball class since motion and force can only be determined once we know what kind of ball it is. The functions only purpose are for usage in inheritance and polymorphism. Since we don't know how to define the functions in class Ball, but still want to use them for inheritance purposes, we need to make them pure virtual. Since at least one member function is pure virtual, the Ball class becomes an abstract base class. The functions motion() and calcForce() are then defined in the derived classes.

```
Ball *b = new Ball(); //error

Ball *b1 = new football();//ok

Ball *b2 = new baseball(); //ok

b1->motion(); //football's function called

b2->motion(); //baseball's function called
```

Search & Sort Examples

Sequention Search / Linear Search:

```
int array[100];

int i=0;

while(array[i]!=mynum){
        i++;
}
```

Complexity: O(n)

Binary Search:

(list/array must be sorted prior to perform binary search from lowest to highest value)

-divide and conquer technique

1) set first(variable) as index 0

2) set last(variable) to last index (size-1)

3)calculate mid(variable) as (first+last)/2

```
if(array[mid]==value){

        found=true;

}

₂else if(value>array[mid]){

        first = mid+1;

}

else{

        last = mid-1;

}
```

Then continue to #3 (third step)

Complexity: $O(\log_2 n)$

Bubble Sort:

```
int temp;

for(int i=1; i<length; i++){

        for(int j=0; j<length-i; j++){

                if(array[j]>array[j+1]){
```

```
            temp = array[j];

            array[j] = array[j+1];

            array[j+1] = temp;

        }

    }

}
```

Linked List

A linked list is a type of data structure made up of nodes that hold data and connect to other nodes. A linked list is different than an array because it is dynamic and can change size. Each node holds the address of the next node. The two items per node are data (the object pointed to by the node) and a link (address of the next node). The address of the first node is held elsewhere.

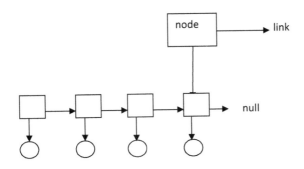

Each node is a class.

```
class node{

public:
```

```cpp
        node(int x, int y);

        node *next;

        data *d;

};
/////////////////////////////////////////////
node::node(int x, int y){

        d=new data(x,y);

        next=null;

}
/////////////////////////////////////////////
class data{
public:

        data(int x, int y);

        int q;

        int r;

};
/////////////////////////////////////////////
data::data(int x, int y){

        q=x;

        r=y;

}
/////////////////////////////////////////////
node *head = new node(1,2);

node *current;

current = head; //used to iterate through the list
```

A Game Development Primer|

```
int s = current->d->q; //get the data

int t = current->d->r; //get the data


create the first node:

node *head = new node(1,2)

current = head;


To add a new node:

node *n1 = new node(5,4);

current->next = n1;

current = n1;


Add another node:

node *n2 = new node(3,3);

current->next = n2;

current = n2;


To search the list:

current = head;

found=false;

while(current!=null && !found){

        if(current->d->q==myVal){

                found=true;

        }

        else{
```

```
            current = current->next;

        }

    }
    node *nodeFound;

    nodeFound = current;

    cout<<nodeFound->d->q<<endl;
```

Complexity: O(n)

Inserting the first node:
```
node *newNode = node(3,4);

newNode->next = head;

head = newNode;
```

Inserting inside the list:
```
node *newNode2 = node(13,2);
```
a) Do a search for node for where to insert

b) make it the current node

then:
```
newNode2->next = current->next;

current->next = newNode2;

current=newNode2;
```

Deleting the first node:
```
node *temp;
```

```
temp =head;

node n = new node(3,3);

n->next = temp->next;

head = n;

delete temp;
```

Deleting the last node:

```
while(current->next!=null){

        current = current->next;

}

delete current->next;

 current->next = null;
```

Deleting an intermediate node:

-first search for node, then

```
node *temp;

temp = current->next;

current->next = current->next->next;

delete temp;
```

Double Linked Lists

The difference between a linked listed and a double linked list is that the latter has a pointer to the previous node also, not just the next. This also means the previous node to the start node points to null, and the next node of the last node points to null.

```
class node{
public:
        node(int x, int y);
        node *next;
        node *prev;
        data *d;
};
```

//

(data class same as before)

//

```
node::node(int x, int y){
        data(x,y);
        next=null;
        prev=null;
}
```

//

```
node *head = new node(4,4);
```

Adding a new node:

```
node *n1 = new node(5,5);
head->next = n1;
n1->prev = head;
```

Adding another node:

```
node *n2 = new node(7,7);
node *current;
```

```
current = head;

while(current->next!=null){

        current = current->next;

}

Current->next = n2;

n2->prev = current;
```

Search Complexity: O(n/2)

Hash Tables

A hash table is simply using an array as a table. To use a hash table a hash formula is required that uses the modulus operator (%) that finds the location based on input.

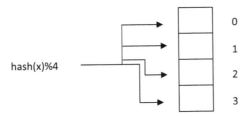

The hash function can be used to insert, delete, or retrieve data. If the hash function is:

```
int hash(int x){

        return x+10;

}
```

Using it in an array of five elements:

int y = hash(131)%5; //141%5 = 1

then:

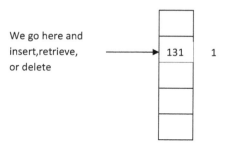

We go here and insert,retrieve, or delete ———→ 131   1

The input to the hash is the data stored in the data structure. This way the data can be retrieved by using its value in the hash function. Furthermore, the array can be extended to hold pointers to linked lists. When inserting data using a hash function, collisions may occur where data already exists in the hashed location. If this occurs, the same input should be used in a rehash function (possibly by adding 1 to the input to find a free location).

Ex:

int counter = 1;

int hash(int x){

        return x+10;

}

//if collision then rehash...

int rehash(int x){

        return x+10+counter;

}

If there is a collision again, increment the counter and use rehash again. When an empty location is found, set the counter back to one an start using the original hash function instead of rehash till another collision occurs.

Const, Mutable, and Friend

The keyword 'const' is used so that the value of what it is applied to cannot change. For variables const can be used but the variable needs to be defined during declaration.

const int y = 5;

y=23;//error

Classes can have const member variables or member functions. Furthermore, const can be used in the parameter to the function implying the function cannot change the parameter. Const member function cannot change the object or any part of it.

Ex:

class A{

public:

 A();

 void myfunc() const; //this function cannot change the object

 char *myfunc2(const char *c);

private:

 int x;

 int y;

};

///

void A::myfunc() const{

 cout<<x<<endl; //doesn't change the value of the class's member

}

char * A::myfunc2(const char *c){

 char a[10];

 strcpy(a,c); //doesn't change c

```
        return a;

}
```

Mutable is a keyword that when used, it means that the variable can change in a function even if the function is 'const'.

Ex:

```
class B{

public:

        B();

        void myfunc(int x) const;

private:

        mutable int y;

};
//////////////////////////////////////////
void B::myfunc(int x) const{

        y++; //this is ok since y is mutable

        return y;

}
```

In classes, one class can be made a 'friend' of another class. The friend class can access private member variables of the class it is defined in.

Ex:

```
class B; //declare the class before defining it so the compiler does not give an error for (1)

class A{

public:

        friend class B; //(1)
```

```
private:

        int x;

        bool y;

};


class  B{

public:

        void myfunc(){

                if(a->x>10){

                        a->y=true;

                }

                else{

                        a->y=false;

                }

        }

private:

        A *a;

};
```

Exception Handling

Exception handling is used to safely handle errors in code. An exception is thrown when the code does not know how to deal with the error that has occurred at runtime. For handling exceptions, a 'try' block is used where the code will 'throw' an exception and the code will also 'catch' the exception to handle it.

```
try{

        if(x==y){

                throw exception();

        }

}

catch(exception e){

        cout<<e.what;

}
```

The steps to set up a 'try' block are:

1) Surround the code where you are checking for errors with try{...}
2) Inside the try block, throw a particular exception based on an event
3) After the try block, if an exception is thrown, the exception is matched with the catch{...} handler. There can be more than one catch block per try block since different exceptions can be thrown in a try block. If there is no match, the program will terminate.

Templates

Templates are used for functions and classes. They are very powerful to make functions and classes more generic, and then later on, become specific.

Function Templates:

```
template<class T> //this is required before the function using the template

void PrintArray(T *array, int count){

        for(int i=0; i<count; i++){

                cout<<array[i]<<endl;

        }

}
```

```
int main(){

        int a_count = 5;

        int b_count = 7;

        int array1[a_count]={1,2,3,4,5};

        char array2[b_count]={'a','b', 'c', 'd', 'e', 'f', 'g'};

        PrintArray(array1, a_count); //T in the function is replaced with int

        PrintArray(array2, b_count);//T in the function is replace with char

        return 1;

}
```

An array of any data type could be passed in to the function since a template was used where T could be of any data type.

Class Templates:

        Class templates are similar to function templates but are used for the class instead of the function.

Ex:

```
template<class T>

class car{

public:

        car();

        T getSpeed();

        void setSpeed(T value);

private:

        T speed;

};
```

```
/////////////////////////////////////////////
template<class T>

car<T>::car(){}


template<class T>

T car<T>::getSpeed(){

        return speed;

}


template<class T>

void car<T>::setSpeed(T value){

        speed = value;

}
/////////////////////////////////////////////
int main(){

        car<int> intspeedcar; //replaces T with int

        int x=25;

        int y;

        intspeedcar.setSpeed(x); //x is int and T is int so correct

        y = intspeedcar.getSpeed();


        car<double> doublespeedcar;

        double x2=34.5;

        double y2;

        doublespeedcar.setSpeed(x2);
```

```
y2 = doublespeedcar.getSpeed();

return 1;
```

}

Useful Functions

a) itoa() – converts an integer to string
b) atoi() – converts a string to an integer
c) memcpy() – copies bytes from one structure to another structure
d) sizeof() – returns number of bytes of a structure

Chapter 5: 3D Graphics Introduction

Over the years, computer graphics has evolved tremendously. It has changed the way we view games by creating an immensely realistic environment that enhances the immersive experience. In this chapter we will be covering various topics in computer graphics.

Colors are essential buildings blocks in computer graphics. The color cube is a good model to understanding red, green, and blue (R,G,B) color values used in computer graphics. Every possible color is some combination of R,G,B values.

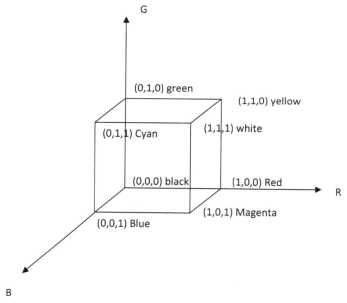

R,G,B values range from 0 to 255. Many times, these values are normalized, like in the color cube. Normalizing the values places them in the range between 0 and 1. Thus, the actual R,G,B value would be divided by 255 to get the normalized value.

Another essential building block of 3D graphics is the coordinate system. Different systems implement the coordinate system slightly differently. OpenGL uses the right-hand rule coordinate system whereas Direct3D implements the left-hand rule coordinate system.

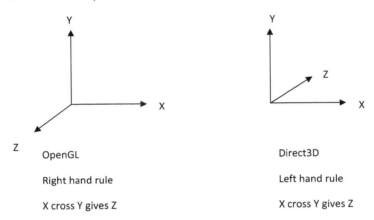

OpenGL	Direct3D
Right hand rule	Left hand rule
X cross Y gives Z	X cross Y gives Z

The graphics hardware architecture is the pipeline through which the graphics flow from software commands to the screen.

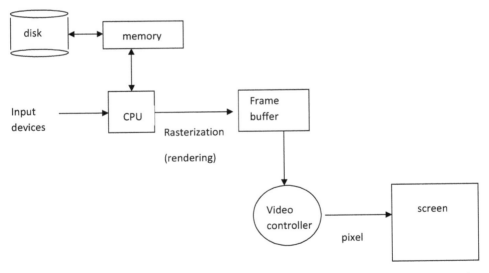

For animation to occur, the frame buffer gets updated. For smooth animation, the frame buffer needs to have a refresh rate of 10-25 frames per second. For 3D graphics, a z-buffer is required. The z-buffer is also known as the depth buffer. It determines which geometrical object is closest to the camera so the non-blocked pixels are rendered.

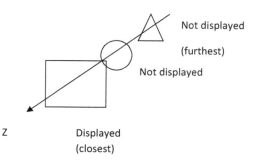

Not displayed
(furthest)

Not displayed

Z   Displayed
           (closest)

Transformations

For creating objects in 3D graphics basic geometric components are used. Usually these are points, triangles, lines, or polygons. Each of these components has at least one vertex. In 3D, a vertex is made of 3 values corresponding to its x, y, and z location in 3-space. In addition to these primitive, moving objects in 3-space is based on three main transformations. The transformations are translation, or moving the object from one location to another, scaling, or resizing the object, and rotating, or turning the object about a particular axis.

Translation:

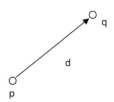

q

d

p

$d = (dx, dy, dz)$

$$p = \begin{bmatrix} x \\ y \\ z \end{bmatrix} \qquad q = \begin{bmatrix} x \\ y \\ z \end{bmatrix} + \begin{bmatrix} dx \\ dy \\ dz \end{bmatrix} = \begin{bmatrix} x+dx \\ y+dy \\ z+dz \end{bmatrix}$$

$$ \qquad\qquad\quad p \qquad\qquad\quad d \qquad\qquad\quad q$$

Most graphics programming APIs require 4 values instead of 3. The last value denotes whether the first 3 values represent a point or a vector. In OpenGL a fourth value of 1 denotes that the 3 values represent a point, whereas if it was 0, the values represent a vector. Furthermore, all transformations are calculated using a transformation matrix. So for translation:

$$q = \begin{bmatrix} x+dx \\ y+dy \\ z+dz \\ 1 \end{bmatrix} = \begin{bmatrix} 1 & 0 & 0 & dx \\ 0 & 1 & 0 & dy \\ 0 & 0 & 1 & dz \\ 0 & 0 & 0 & 1 \end{bmatrix} \begin{bmatrix} x \\ y \\ z \\ 1 \end{bmatrix}$$

$$\qquad\qquad\qquad\qquad\qquad\qquad\qquad\qquad\qquad p$$

Where: x + dx = ax + by + cz + d

Scale:

$$p \begin{bmatrix} x \\ y \\ z \\ 1 \end{bmatrix} \xrightarrow{\ s(dx\ dy\ dz)\ } \begin{bmatrix} dx*x \\ dy*y \\ dz*z \\ 1 \end{bmatrix}$$

$$\qquad\qquad\qquad\qquad\qquad q$$

$$\begin{bmatrix} dx * x \\ dy*y \\ dx*z \\ 1 \end{bmatrix} = \begin{bmatrix} \alpha_x & 0 & 0 & 0 \\ 0 & \alpha_y & 0 & 0 \\ 0 & 0 & \alpha_z & 0 \\ 0 & 0 & 0 & 1 \end{bmatrix} \begin{bmatrix} x \\ y \\ z \\ 1 \end{bmatrix}$$

Rotation:

$$P = \begin{matrix} x \\ y \\ z \end{matrix} = \begin{matrix} r*\cos\Phi \\ r*\sin\Phi \\ z \end{matrix}$$

$$q = \begin{matrix} r*\cos(\Theta+\Phi) \\ r*\sin(\Theta+\Phi) \\ z \end{matrix} = \begin{matrix} r*(\cos\Phi\cos\Theta - \sin\Phi\sin\Theta) \\ r*(\sin\Phi\cos\Theta + \cos\Phi\sin\Theta) \\ z \end{matrix}$$

$$q = \begin{bmatrix} (\cos\Theta)x + (-\sin\Theta)y \\ (\sin)x + (\cos)y \\ z \\ 1 \end{bmatrix} = \begin{bmatrix} \cos\Theta & -\sin\Theta & 0 & 0 \\ \sin\Theta & \cos\Theta & 0 & 0 \\ 0 & 0 & 1 & 0 \\ 0 & 0 & 0 & 1 \end{bmatrix} \begin{bmatrix} x \\ y \\ z \\ 1 \end{bmatrix}$$

When there are multiple transformations, the transformation matrix is constructed to include all the transformations and then multiplied by the point it is being applied to. An identity matrix is used when there are no transformations.

Identity Matrix:

1	0	0	0
0	1	0	0
0	0	1	0
0	0	0	1

For animation, a concept known as double buffering is used. The way double buffering works is that the final image is drawn to the buffer. After this, the buffer "swaps" to the screen. As the image is displayed on the screen, a new image is drawn to the buffer and then a "swap" occurs and the process continues.

Lighting and Shading

A 3D scene is incomplete without lighting and materials used to calculate the color of a pixel based on the lighting in the scene. There are three types of surfaces that geometrical objects can have; specular, diffuse, and translucent. There are also four types of light sources; ambient, point source, spotlight, and distant light. The lighting and shading add realism to the 3D scene. The light reflects off the material and hits the eye, so the end result of what you see is based on the light source and the material.

Ambient light is used for a constant light from all directions throughout the scene. Therefore every point is illuminated by the same amount. It is also important to know that lights also have R,B,G values and therefore can emit light of a particular color.

A point source light emits light equally in all directions from a particular point, and therefore has a location for the source. The source has an x,y, and z coordinate. However, the light intensity decreases with distance and therefore an object closer to the point source light will be illuminated more than one that is further away. The intensity is inversely proportional to the distance squared. If we wanted to find out the intensity at some point P in the scene with a point source light P_0:

$I(P, P_0) = (1/|P - P_0|)*I(P_0)$

$d = |P - P_0|$

$I(P, P_0) = (1/d^2)*I(P_0)$

Where

$$I(P_0) = \begin{array}{l} I_r(P_0) \\ I_g(P_0) \\ I_b(P_0) \end{array}$$

A spotlight has a location and color and a narrow range of angles through which light is emitted.

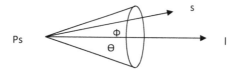

Θ is the max angle of the lighting range. If Θ is 180 degrees, then the spotlight becomes a point source light. The intensity is proportional to $\cos\Phi$ to the power e which is the angular falloff coefficient. Also, $\cos\Phi$ is the dot product of s and I. A distant light is similar to a point source light except has a constant direction and is a vector as opposed to a point as the point source light.

Surface types have been mentioned, but there are also three types of light-material interaction; ambient, diffuse, and specular. This interaction is basically how the pixel is shaded based on how the light reflects off the surface. One model that calculates this is the Phong reflection model, also considered to be pixel shading.

Phong reflection model:

4 vectors used

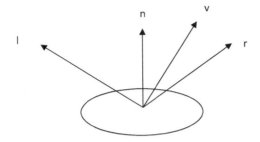

l – light source

n – normal

v - camera

r – perfect reflection

The normal vector is required for all lighting and shading and is a vector that is perpendicular to the surface. To calculate the surface normal the cross product is taken of two edges of the surface polygon that share a vertex.

In the Phong reflection model the illumination at a point has an ambient, diffuse and specular component for each R,G,B value.

Iir   =   Iira   +   Iird   +   Iirs

Where I is the illumination, i is the light source, r is red, a is ambient, d is diffuse, and s is specular. The similar calculation is done for green and blue components.

Ambient Reflection:

Ia =La * Ka

Where La is the light source ambient value and Ka is the material ambient value.

(separate calculations for r,g,b)

Diffuse Reflection:

(rough surface, light scatters)

$Id = (I \bullet n)Ld * Kd$

Specular reflection:

(reflective, shiny)

$Is = (r \bullet v)^{\alpha}Ks * Ls$

Where α is the shininess coefficient and the surface becomes a mirror as it tends to infinity.

In OpenGL and Direct3D objects can use flat shading or smooth shading. For flat shading, the surface normal is used to calculate the illumination of the pixels of the polygon (all the pixels of the polygon will have the same illumination). Smooth shading calculates the vertex illumination using the vertex normal and then calculates the illumination of the polygon pixels by interpolation.

Viewing

For viewing the 3D scene, cameras are used. From the "camera" to rendering to the screen, to position and orientation of the camera must be defined, and then the scene goes through a projection matrix and then a viewport transformation before finally being rendered. There are two types of projection; parallel (orthogonal) and perspective. The viewport transformation does the calculation of where to draw the pixels on the screen.

Camera position and orientation:

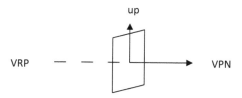

VRP is the view reference point (camera position)

VPN is the view plane normal (line of sight)

up is a direction vector that represents the camera orientation.

Projection:

Perspective projection   orthogonal projection

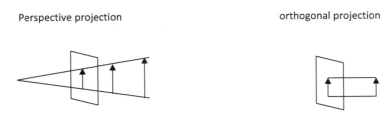

Camera:

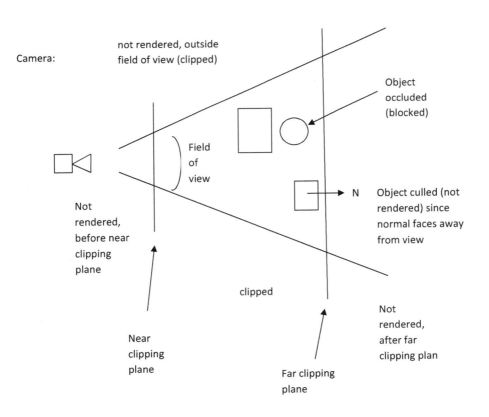

not rendered, outside field of view (clipped)

Object occluded (blocked)

Field of view

N   Object culled (not rendered) since normal faces away from view

Not rendered, before near clipping plane

clipped

Not rendered, after far clipping plan

Near clipping plane

Far clipping plane

Texture Mapping

Textures maps are 2D images that are applied to 3D models. This can greatly increase the realism of a scene without the need for extra polygons. The texture map used should match the "look" and "feel" of the level being designed. Some common file formats for textures are .tga, .tiff, .png, .bmp, and .jpg.

Texture maps have their own set of coordinates, usually denoted as UV. Each polygons x, y, and z vertex is assigned to a UV coordinate, thus mapping the 2D to 3D. In 3D graphics software, the vertices UV coordinates are determined by first "unwrapping" the 3D model to a 2D plane. The texture is overlayed on the 2D plane to see where the texture pixels fall on the unwrapped 3D model. Once the UVs are assigned, the 3D model will be textured accordingly.

There are different ways to map the UV coordinates. Projection mapping is the most common. One type of projection mapping is planar mapping. This is where the texture is projected to a plane. Box mapping projects the texture on six sides. Cylindrical mapping is a wrapped planar map, which is useful when texture mapping a character's face or arm. Finally, there is also spherical mapping. All these methods create new UVs for geometry, but many times, the UVs need to be tweaked to fit the model which is done manually. So the process is:

1) create new UVs by unwrapping the model
2) tweak the UVs
3) create the texture to fit the UV mapping
4) wrap the model back and place the texture

Tiling is a method that is highly used when texturing levels and terrains. Tiling is where the texture image is repeated over surfaces. However, a problem with this is that irregularities can occur at the seams of the texture. The solution is to make the texture map edges such that if the same texture is placed next to it, it will flow and be continuous.

Mip-mapping is another common technique. It is used so that memory is used efficiently as texture mapping can be resource intensive. Mipmaps use the original texture at its original resolution and then create copies of the same texture at lower and lower resolutions and these are stored in a data structure. The Mipmaps are then used dynamically where the higher resolution texture is used when the object is close to the camera and lower resolution textures used as the object gets further from the camera. This is a viable solution since when the object is far away, a high resolution texture is not needed.

Environment mapping is a technique where a texture map broken into six pieces, or cube map, is applied to a reflective surface in a scene. The images in each of the six pieces of the cube map are snapshots of the world from a location in different directions. Thus, when applied to an object in the center of the world, gives the illusion of reflection.

Bump mapping is a process where the surface normals are skewed so that when shaded, it makes the surface seem rough or bumpy. On a flat surface, if all the normals face in the same direction, the reflection angle of light rays would be the same. If the normals were slighted skewed in various directions, the light rays would be reflected in different angles also and therefore make the surface seem bumpy.

Polygon Notes

The polygon most commonly used in 3D models is a triangle. Thus, the entire 3D scene can all be made up of many triangles. The more triangles used, the more realistic the scene looks. However, as the polygon count increases, more memory is used and the real-time rendering time slows down.

As a designer, you must decide how many polygons to use for a 3D model. This decision should be based on how fast should the game run in frames per second, how realistic should it look, how much memory should it use, and what is the limit that the game engine can handle.

There are techniques used to reduce the polygon count without sacrificing realism. For example, if a plane has a lot of tessellation, where it is subdivided into many triangles, and does not require it, polygons can be reduced for that plane. Another way to reduce polygon count is that if a face (surface of a polygon) is not seen in the game (ever), then the face can be deleted. An example of this is if a non-movable barrel was on the ground, the bottom of the barrel is never seen, and therefore the face of the bottom of the barrel can be deleted. These types of reduction techniques help increase the frames per second rendering speed and thus provide smoother animations.

Chapter 6: Audio in Games

Audio is vital component for games. Over time, audio has evolved as now there are better sound cards, faster processors, better codecs for more efficient compression and decompression, and more memory as sound files can prove to have a large memory footprint.

Sound can also be 2D or 3D. 2D sound is also considered ambient sound and is the same everywhere in the scene. 3D sound has a source position which is called an emitter. As the emitter moves, the sound also moves by varying the amplitude of the wave signal.

Analog to Digital

Sound waves are analog signals. This means they are continuous and non-discrete. For digital electronics to understand and process the signal, they need to be converted to digital. This is done via sampling. Samples of the analog signals are taken at a certain rate or frequency. The higher the sampling rate, the more closely the digital data represents the original analog signal. The sampling rate can go up to 44.1 kHz and each sample can be made up of a certain number of bits. The higher the bits per sample, the better quality the audio will be in digital format. For example, each sample can be 128 bits.

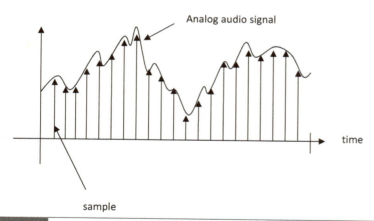

Analog audio signal

time

sample

An example for sampling would be to sample at 8 kHz, or 8000 samples per second, with 8 bits per sample and the audio waveform has a 2 second duration. With this, there would be 16,000 samples (8000 * 2) and the number of bits required for the 2 seconds of audio would be 128,000 bits (16,000 * 8). If the waveforms highest frequency was 16 kHz, then we have sampled at a frequency less than the signal's highest frequency. The problem with this is that when the analog signal is reconstructed from digital data (when sending the electrical signal to speakers for example), then the reconstructed signal will not be the same as the original waveform or accurately represent it. The solution to this is to sample at the Nyquist rate. The Nyquist rate is twice the highest frequency of the original signal. When this is done, when the signal is reconstructed, it will be the same as the original waveform.

(frequency is number of cycles per second)

3D Sound

3D sound requires an emitter at a location in a 3D scene. Depending on where it is placed in the world, a certain frequency is heard. If the emitter is stationary, then all listeners hear the same frequency (change in pitch). If the emitter is moving, then the sound will be heard as a lower frequency to listeners from which the emitter is moving away from, and as a higher frequency for listeners where the emitter is moving towards. This is known as the Doppler Effect. The reason why the sound is heard as a higher frequency if it is moving toward you is because the sound compresses. If it is moving away from you, it expands.

The roll-off factor is how quickly the sound diminishes as it radiates from its source with respect to distance. A value of 0 means no attenuation. A value of 1 is real-world attenuation. A value higher than 1 is increased attenuation.

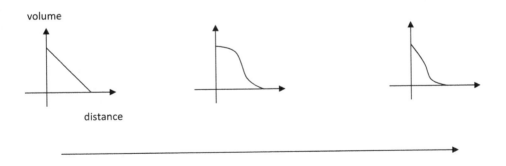

Increased roll-off factor

The distance factor is where the further you listener is from the source, the sound gets software in terms of volume. If the listener moves within a minimum distance from the audio emitter, the sound volume, which is measured in decibels (dB), does not change and stays at maximum. After this distance, the sound volume begins to decrease at a rate depending on the roll-off factor. An important equation for 3D sound is:

Attenuation (dB) = 20 * $\log_{10}(R/r)$

Where R is the reference distance and r is the actual distance.

It is important to know that sound has direction. Consider a person talking. The sound from his mouth travels is a particular direction. Ambient sound is different than 3D sound. Ambient sound can be heard equally from everywhere. An example of ambient sound would be looping background music for a level. Stereo sound is where the sound is broken into channels and sound can come from the left speaker, right speaker, or both. The method used for changing the volume of sound for the left or right speaker is known as panning.

Signal Domains

There are three types of audio effects, or domains. The first is the time domain, the second is the frequency domain, and the third is the amplitude domain. In the time domain, this where there is a certain time duration before the sound reaches the listener from the time it was emitted. Sound can also take different paths and therefore can reach the listener at different time intervals. An example of this would be multiple echoes when shouting in a canyon. Some other effects in the time domain are reverb and chorus.

Sound in the frequency domain has a fundamental plus harmonics. The fundamental is a sine wave and the harmonics are additional sine waves which are of different frequencies than the fundamental, but are higher multiples of the fundamental. For example, a piano note will have a fundamental plus harmonics.

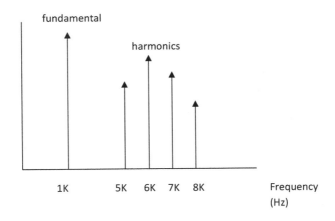

Different filters can be used in the frequency domain. A high-pass filter only allows frequencies above a given value to pass. Similarly, a low-pass filter only allows lower frequencies to pass. Finally, a band-pass filter will only allow a certain bandwidth of frequencies to pass. For example, a band-pass filter may only allow frequencies between 20kHz and 30kHz to pass.

The final domain for signals is the amplitude domain. This is simply an increase or decrease in volume in decibels (dB). An example of a special effect in the amplitude domain would be distortion.

Emotion Engineering with Audio

The emotions of a player can be engineered by the music in a game to some degree. Music is a powerful tool to surface different emotions. A composer knows this and creates music to create a certain mood for the listener. In games, different music is used at different times, places, and for different reasons. For example, interactive music changes based on what the player's actions are, whether it is during combat or exploring the level.

The music used will be different for the game intro, the closing or conclusion, and the credits. During the intro sequence, this is the first time the players hears music. It is intended to build excitement, set the mood, and establish the story. It creates the players first impression. During the closing cut-scene, the music should provide closure and make the player feel rewarded for winning the game. During the credits, the music should be background music.

A cut-scene's purpose is not only to drive the story, but uses music also for various purposes. The music during a cut-scene will also create the mood, set the pace, and still highlight the plot. Sometimes it can be used to create tension or excitement. Music for cut-scenes is designed and created to be linear, like film.

Music also has purpose during the menu screen. The music may also be different depending on when the menu screen is viewed. For the initial menu screen the music can create emotions for the "calm before the storm" and to build interest and excitement for playing the game. Thus, the mood is set and a feeling of the type of game, in regards to the story, actions, and settings, is created. During a game menu, the music could represent a "rest" station, and the pseudo-background music simply loops.

The music during gameplay is a vital tool. Depending on the game genre, different types of music would be used. For example, if the game was a car racing game, the music would be upbeat and loud. The soundtrack used for gameplay is looped. There may be multiple soundtracks, or clips, that can alternate and the combination looped. For example, as the player gets closer to the boss, the music can get more intense and faster. In sports games, however, many times music is not used but replaced with commentary during gameplay.

Music also serves to advance the plot in the sense that it changes based on the events of the game. There are transition cues both audio and visual such as in cut-scenes. If there is no cut-scene at a particular part of the game, then music can be used to setup what's to come as a tool for foreshadowing.

Music is also tied to "winning" and "losing". If the player is winning, the music should be optimistic and have a rewarding sound as recognition of victory. If the player is losing, the music should be encouraging to the player to try harder or try again.

Interactive music is comprised of various musical clips that can play at any time based on the in-game events. It is important that the clips blend well into each other. It should be used to change the mood of the player. For example, when the player is exploring, slow and surreal sounds can be used. When changing from walking to running, the tempo of the clip may pick up. If danger is approaching, clips that increase tension can be used. If a weapon is picked up, clips that portray battle can be used.

Chapter 7: Networks and Games

Games can be local or online. Online games have become more popular due to the advancements in networks and the internet. Many online games have their own genre such as Massively Multiplayer Online Role Playing Games, or Massively Multiplayer Online Real Time Strategy. However, with networked games, there are some challenges. This chapter discusses some of these challenges and solutions to these challenges.

In local games, there is fine control over events and interactions. The model is to receive input, update the sprites, perform collision detection, and to render the graphics. The speed of this loop can be controlled by code based on the hardware. Also, synchronization is not an issue.

When creating online games, or LAN based games, network API are required for programming. But before this, the designer needs to decide whether the game will use the UDP network protocol, or the TCP protocol. UDP is a connectionless protocol that is fast, but unreliable. It is unreliable in the sense that network packets may be dropped. TCP is a connection oriented protocol that is reliable, but slow. In real-time games TCP is commonly used but the problem is that delays are introduced by the nature of the TCP protocol.

The greatest challenges in networked games are latency (delays) and bandwidth. The goal of the designer is to get good performance and consistent synchronization by providing fast and reliable data transfer. The question arises as to how to design the netcode to use TCP but also decrease the latency.

Latency

Network latency can make or break online games. Data transfer that is required is for updating players for logic, and updating the world for consistency so that what one player sees, the other player sees the same thing. An average of a 300ms round-trip-time (RTT) will greatly affect the game as jumps and pauses will occur. The goal is to minimize this delay. For example, if the game runs at 30 frames per second (fps), with 35 to 50 milliseconds between frames, and the internet delay is 100 ms, and the processing delay is 200 ms, and there are packet loss delays, then the game will stall for greater than or equal to 5 frames.

There are different types of network delays. One type is propagation delay. Propagation delays are based on the hardware medium of communication, such as electrical wires or fiber optics. Not much improvement can be made for propagation delay except to replace all wires with fiber optics. Another type of delay is queuing delay where packets are queued before transmission. This occurs at the router or switch. Processing delays are due to modems or Ethernet cards. Software buffering may also introduce delays.

Bandwidth

Online games require large spurts of data and therefore more bandwidth. The bandwidth available is also directly related to timing. Higher bandwidth consumption means higher delays due to flow control. Also, the more packets sent, the more chances there are of the packets being dropped or queued behind packets of other users.

However, there are techniques that can be used to solve this problem. One technique is data compression. The flow of using compression would be to compress the data, create the packet, send the packet, and decompress the packet at the receiving end.

Another technique is packet aggregation. Packet aggregation is creating a larger packet from smaller packets so that there is only one header packet.

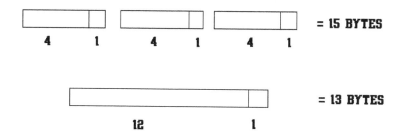

A third technique is interest management where packets are only sent to relevant clients. An example of interest management for a first person shooter is only send packets that are relevant to the field of view of the player, send the packet only if the player is in the field of view of another player. This means that packets that affect the part of the world that is not in the field of view of the player do not need to be sent as they are irrelevant.

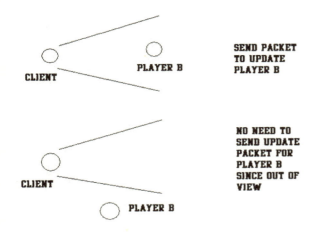

SEND PACKET
TO UPDATE
PLAYER B

NO NEED TO
SEND UPDATE
PACKET FOR
PLAYER B
SINCE OUT OF
VIEW

Other Optimizations

Updating the player position can pose a problem as it needs to be updated every frame but this may not be possible due to network delays. The solution to this is to use data extrapolation. Data extrapolation is based on previous locations and previous timestamps. From this, a polynomial equation can be used to extrapolate an expected new position. For example:

T = timestamp

P = position

Polynomial equation for parabolic curve:

$P(T) = aT^2 + bT + c$

$P0x = ax*T0^2 + bx*T0 + cx$

$P1x = ax*T1^2 + bx*T1 + cx$

$P2x = ax*T2^2 + bx*T2 + cx$

(we know P0,P1,P2 and T0,T1,T2 -> solve for ax,bx,cx)

$Px(T) = ax*T^2 + bx*T + c$

$Pz(T) = az*T^2 + bz*T + c$

Can calculate the new position at a given time

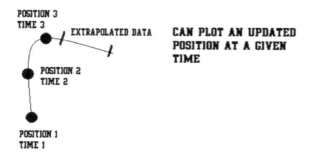

For online multiplayer games, the world needs to be the same for all players.   For this to happen, data needs to be sent to all clients at a fast rate and at the same speed. The probability of this occurring on the internet is low.   Even if the world can be kept in sync, the players need to be updated as well.   The solution to this and also to reduce the amount of bandwidth required is only send packets when a state-change has occurred.   Instead of sending explicit player information, such as the player's current position, state-change messages are sent.   However, this can only be done on deterministic systems.   Examples are if the player presses X to jump, or the left arrow to move left.

Example:

Update player's position per packet

        (0,0,0)

        (1,0,0)

        (2,0,0)

        (3,0,0)

        (3,1,0)

        (3,2,0)

        (3,3,0)

=7 packets

versus

Update player's position based on state change per packet

Right arrow pressed (player is moving right)

Up arrow pressed (player is moving up)

=2 packets

With the player's current position and current velocity, the new position can be calculated locally based on the state-change event packet. Finally, the real-time network protocol can be used for voice and video streaming. Real-time protocol is most commonly used on a multicast system for Voice over IP (VoIP).

Appendix

Common Game Development Documents

1) Pitch document / One-pager / Concept document
2) Production Plan
3) Storyboard
4) Game Design Document
5) Technical Design Document
6) Post-mortem

Common Game Development Tools

1) Microsoft Visual Studio or other IDE
2) 3D studio Max or Maya or other 3D modeling software
3) Game Engine
4) Audio tools
5) Video creation and editing tools
6) Word processor and document creation software
7) Motion Capture System
8) Version control software
9) In-house created tools used for development